THE
KEEP IT SHORT & SIMPLE
Party Menu Book

Ruth H. Brent

THE Keep It Short & Simple Party Menu Book

HOLT, RINEHART AND WINSTON

New York   Chicago   San Francisco

Published simultaneously in Canada by Holt, Rinehart
and Winston of Canada, Limited.

Library of Congress Cataloging in Publication Data

BRENT, RUTH H.
 The keep it short & simple party menu book.
 1. Entertaining. 2. Menus. 3. Cookery. I. Title.
TX731.B68   641.5'68   72-78137
ISBN 0-03-091885-5

FIRST EDITION

Designer: Ernst Reichl
Printed in the United States of America

For my husband, Harrison, who enjoys
"having friends in" as much as I do

Contents

Author's Note

The word "hospitality" is defined as "the cordial and generous reception of guests." It isn't fine appointments or elaborate food which is necessary. It's the spirit which counts—the willingness and desire to share whatever we have, no matter how humble our home.

Home entertaining is one of the great privileges and joys of life. While we're young, whether married or single, we should get into the habit of having friends and family in often. It not only gives other people a great deal of happiness, but a lot of it will brush off on us.

The Keep It Short & Simple Party Menu Book contains 101 tips for unforgettable parties which you can duplicate in your own home. Organized by season, the parties should be easy to work with because they are all presented uniformly: First are suggestions for invitations; next are appetizing menus, complete with tips for preparing and serving each dish, followed by short, simple recipes, most requiring no more than four ingredients.

I'd like to call attention to the recipes themselves. Many were sent by family and friends and I'm most grateful to them. All recipes have been tested in my own kitchen. In addition to the delightful fact that they call for very few ingredients, the recipes are all easy to follow. Much more detailed information is given than in the average recipe. The number of servings is clearly stated at the top as is a list of equipment needed; name brands are recommended where advisable.

The section in each party called "Tips for Preparing and Serving" is enormously helpful.

A section titled "Setting the Scene" gives helpful pointers for establishing a festive party atmosphere, including decorations and suitable table settings.

Entertaining games are included wherever appropriate. Occasions such as Halloween, Valentine's Day, Fourth of July, bridal showers, and children's parties all cry out for after-supper fun.

Warm-hearted hostesses avoid giving large impersonal parties merely to pay off obligations. Instead they entertain frequently at cozy intimate parties for a few friends. Entertaining is fun but remember keep it short and simple!

Ruth H. Brent

Downey, California
October 1973

Introduction
to Party Planning

Introduction

Most of us need instruction in party giving, as we do in any other accomplishment. There are preparations and procedures to follow which are different from other homemaking tasks. *A woman may be able to afford all the help in the world, but if she herself doesn't know the finer points of entertaining, the chances are that she will never have a successful party.*

Learn how to establish a happy atmosphere. It's easy when you know how and it may all be found in this book.

ENTERTAINING WITH FLAIR

Have you ever noticed that sometimes, the moment you arrive at a party, you sense that it's going to be a great one? Sometimes you aren't even aware of the individual touches that go into establishing this atmosphere, but all of these things have an effect on your emotions: flickering candlelight—lots of it; fresh flowers, attractively arranged; a beautifully set table; arrangement of furniture into cozy groups; soft background music; a crackling fire when it's stormy and cold outside; a freshly aired, fragrant house; and last, but certainly not least, a relaxed and happy host and hostess.

THE HOSTESS

Learning to become a proficient hostess is one of the most rewarding tasks of homemaking. What are the most important qualities in becoming a good hostess?

There are several things on which I place great importance:

· The warm and loving welcome at the door to show friends the hostess is *really* happy that the guests are there.
· The unhurried, serene, and carefree attitudes of both host and hostess, showing by their party mood that they expect to enjoy the evening as much as anyone else.
· The desire to give their guests a wonderfully happy evening which involves introducing guests who have similar interests, attending to such needs as supplying drinks, cigarettes, comfortable seating—in short, seeing to their guests' general welfare.
· The way in which the hostess is dressed. If she is dressed and adorned, the party assumes more importance to all.

"Some women are just born hostesses. When they entertain they do it so easily." We often hear that remark. Don't you believe it! The "born hostess" has worked very hard to achieve this effect. She has organized the party well in advance and has completed almost all preparations before the actual party day.

PARTY PLANNING

Let's discuss briefly specific procedures for giving successful, worry-free parties, ones which the host and hostess will enjoy as much as their guests. You'll notice that I didn't say "work-free." Alas, that isn't possible anymore when the majority of us double as housekeeper, cook, and waitress. We can, however, give the illusion of it all being effortless if we can plan carefully and do everything possible in the days before.

Here, in capsule form, are the important steps of entertaining. So that nothing will be forgotten, map it out first on paper:

1. Type of party, date, and time.
2. Guest list—whether to send written invitations or telephone.
3. Menu. Assemble recipes and make grocery list.
4. Type of before-dinner drinks. Make a list of necessary supplies such as mixes, garnishes, cocktail napkins, soft drinks, ice, etc.

In addition make a shopping list for miscellaneous items like guest towels, flowers, candles, place cards, and prizes.

5. Table setting. Check linens, china, glassware, silver, serving dishes, serving spoons, and forks. Do you need to borrow anything? Make arrangement ahead of time to pick it up.

6. Method of serving. Will it be a buffet or sit-down meal? Make a list of ways in which guests can help. (Take advantage of all those offers, particularly from family and close friends.)

7. Entertainment. Will you play bridge or party games? If so, assemble all equipment well ahead of time.

8. Party attire. Check to make sure that it's ready to wear.

9. Make out detailed schedules for the days before the party and for party day.

Picture just how you want the party to proceed, how you want your house to look, how you want to decorate your table, how you want your food to taste. Your main goal will be to give your guests a wonderfully happy time. Only by having a goal will you be able to stage a party of which you can be proud.

TIPS FOR THE HOSTESS

· In making out your guest list keep in mind that "people make the party." Let's face it, there are many—usually those with very limited interests—whose conversation is far from interesting. If you're a novice hostess, be a little selfish and invite people who give you confidence, people you really like, those you know will enjoy and appreciate your efforts.

· After you've completed your guest list, make two copies. Prop one up on your husband's dresser, one on your own. Glance at it occasionally, particularly on Party Day. You'll find that you'll easily remember everyone's name as you make introductions.

· An out-of-town guest or guest-of-honor should always be introduced to every person, preferably as each arrives. To accomplish this, request that the guest-of-honor arrive a few minutes ahead of time. It's a kindness too if the hostess, in advance, makes a list of expected guests and presents it to the stranger (provided the party isn't too large). In addition she could include a short remark about each such as: Mary Tyler—talented singer; Jack Martin—very sports-minded; Ben Glass—local newscaster.

· Ask one of your close friends to see that the guest-of-honor is provided with a drink and hors d'oeuvres and above all to see that she isn't stranded. It's almost impossible for the host and hostess to do this in addition to their other duties.

TYPES OF PARTIES

Inexperienced hostesses are sometimes under the impression that in order to have a good party it must be a real production with a lot of people, elaborate menu, kitchen help to serve, a roar of conversation and laughter, dance music, and games. Such parties certainly have their place, but so do the small, quiet ones at which you really have an opportunity to get to know people better or to renew old friendships.

Some of the most memorable parties I've ever attended were those for three to six people. These were relaxed, unhurried occasions where we could catch up on all the news and have an opportunity to exchange viewpoints on provocative and interesting subjects. Another advantage of the small party is that the average hostess usually has china, silverware, glassware, and chairs for 6 or 8, so there is no need for excess borrowing. Especially appropriate for a small group is a seated brunch, luncheon or dinner; barbecue supper or pre-theater or after-theater party.

When entertaining a larger group of more than 8, you have a greater selection of parties from which to choose. Here are some of the most popular: morning coffee, buffet brunch or luncheon, dessert and coffee, bridge, committee meeting, picnic, afternoon tea, bridal or baby shower, cocktail party or open house, buffet supper.

FAMILY PARTIES I personally adore family parties. I love parties where the guest list includes infants up to people in their nineties. Some of our happiest childhood memories are of family picnics, Easter and Christmas parties, Fourth of July cookouts.

We are all prone to limit our entertaining to parties for our contemporaries, but the two age groups who enjoy parties most are left out—youngsters and elderly people. Many times grandmothers and grandfathers, elderly aunts and uncles, might go for a year or more without an invitation. This seems grossly unfair as they are the very ones who entertained us when we were small.

CLUB OR GROUP POTLUCK PARTIES The custom of each person or each family contributing an item toward the supper or picnic has been in use for many generations. Neighbors helped one another out for a "barn-raisin'," or when crops needed harvesting or when a house needed painting. In pioneer days, communal projects provided the excuse for the few social "get-togethers," and after the work was done, the enormous potluck supper was spread out on trestle tables.

Today, when help is almost nonexistent, the custom of sharing the responsibility is enjoying new popularity. It enables family, friends, or club members to meet often without too much burden falling on any one person. Particularly appropriate to this kind of entertaining are family parties; class reunions; club committee meetings; fund-raising events; office or company parties.

Several systems are possible:

1. One-third brings a favorite casserole; one-third a favorite salad; one-third a favorite dessert. This makes for a pretty display on a buffet table.
2. A menu is decided on, mimeographed sheets of the entire menu, and recipes are sent to each member, who is requested to bring a specific dish.
3. Couples who meet regularly for dinner and bridge might follow this procedure, rotating courses on successive evenings:

Couple 1 (host and hostess):	Supplies drinks and coffee
Couple 2:	Snacks, dips, and rolls
Couple 3:	Meat course (couples take turns)
Couple 4:	Vegetables
Couple 5:	Salads
Couple 6:	Desserts

Name tags are practically a *must* for club, group, or church parties. Members and visitors alike appreciate them and it is much easier for members of the committee to make introductions.

Also popular and fun are neighborhood and community parties. These can be as simple as a morning coffee to introduce a new neighbor or as complex as a full-scale block party. Pre-party planning where neighbors can get together and work out details are most rewarding insofar as bettering community good will is concerned. For this type of party, the women ordinarily prepare the food, while the men plan and supervise the games; teenagers can be especially helpful at arranging games and in overseeing those for the younger children.

THEMES

Parties with a theme are fun to give and fun to attend.

Hostesses enjoy the challenge of coordinating invitations, menu, table setting, games, and music.

In addition to special holidays such as Thanksgiving, Easter, and Christmas, and occasions like Valentine's Day and Halloween, popular themes for children are: Circus, Pirate, Mother Goose, Train, Cowboys and Indians, Space Ship, Doll's Tea Party.

Away-from-home excursions might be one of these: Picnic, Theater Party, Ball Game, Beach Party, Bicycle Jaunt, Train Ride, Camping Trip, Zoo Visit, Amusement Park Spree.

Good themes for adult parties, in addition to the ones in this book are: Wild West, Gypsy, Mexican Fiesta, Oriental, Roaring Twenties, Hill Billy, Gay Nineties, Pioneer Days, Monte Carlo, Street Carnival, Paris Nights, Italian Street Scene, Patriotic, Scandinavian Smorgasbord, East Indian (Curry), Shipwreck.

Theme parties are especially suitable for large home parties and club or church affairs.

INVITATIONS

The guidelines for an invitation are the same as those of the reporter in writing up a news story. The hostess must answer the questions: Who? What? Where? When? Why? If you'll keep them in mind, you'll find that it is easy to write invitations.

Who: Name of the host, hostess or organization
What: Type of party—luncheon, brunch, or dinner
When: Day of the week, date, and time
Where: Address of the party site, whether at home or at a restaurant or wherever
Why: Reason for party—to entertain a bride-to-be, to meet a friend, to welcome a new neighbor, to discuss a club program (There *needn't* be a why. You may just be in the spirit to get the crowd together.)

Another thing that guests may want to know is, in military parlance, the "uniform of the day." Today, almost anything goes in the way of dress. This is especially true at a cocktail party, and especially true of women guests, as some may be coming in knit suits directly from work or a day of shopping, and others may be in long gowns on their way to a semiformal dinner or the theater.

It doesn't really matter anymore. People dress as they please. If someone calls to ask, you might say, "I'm wearing a long hostess gown, but I'm sure that many will be in street clothes. Just wear whatever's most comfortable," or words to that effect.

TIPS TO REMEMBER ABOUT INVITATIONS

· If the party is in honor of someone, don't forget to include it on the invitation.
· When inviting a couple to an affair, the hostess extends the invitation to the wife. When inviting an unattached man, the hostess drops him a note or calls him personally.
· If your home is difficult to find or your guests have not been there before, it is thoughtful to give clear directions, preferably in writing, or send a small map.
· If gifts are to be given, let everyone know. It is embarrassing to be the only one who has come empty-handed.

cMENU PLANNING

"Keep it short and simple" might well be the slogan for planning party menus. Experienced hostesses seldom plan more than three courses, especially if they must be combination cook, waitress, and hostess. Dinner usually consists of soup *or* salad, an entrée with vegetables, and dessert. Luncheon is usually cut down to two courses, a hearty soup followed by a salad, or a salad plate followed by dessert.

For ease of preparation and serving, consider a one-course meal. As an example, for a ladies' luncheon you could arrange on one plate dainty, open-faced sandwiches, a cup of consomme or cream soup, relishes, and for dessert a bonbon or two in a small paper cup.

Next in importance are recipes which may be prepared ahead of time so that hot foods need only reheating and cold items need only be whisked from refrigerator to table. While still in the planning stage, work out a schedule for which everything is ready at the same time. Above all, avoid recipes that require last minute preparation.

For plate-on-the-lap suppers, plan items which can be managed with a fork alone.

TIPS FOR PLANNING MENUS

· Vegetables and fruits are not only lowest-priced in season, but are at their prime in taste, texture, and color. Do take advantage of the seasons and serve strawberries in May, fresh garden vegetables in midsummer, crunchy cranberry relish in November.
· Take the weather into consideration. A hearty, thick soup tastes ever so good on a stormy day, but a salad lunch is a better choice in midsummer.
· Although it is stimulating to experiment with new menus and recipes, there are special holidays throughout the year when it is more satisfying to follow tradition—heart-shaped desserts on St. Valentine's Day, corned beef and cabbage on St. Patrick's Day, hot cross buns at Easter, turkey at Thanksgiving.

- Avoid using a food in two different ways, such as tomato soup, followed by a stuffed tomato salad.
- Consider color and texture. A menu consisting of creamed fish, mashed potatoes, cauliflower—all white foods—will not have the eye or taste appeal of creamed fish, buttered beets, and green beans with toasted almonds.
- Dramatize your food by using attractive, colorful garnishes. This is especially important when the food is all displayed together for buffet serving.
- When serving a large group, consider offering a choice of desserts on a "sweet trolley," modeled after those seen in many restaurants. Tortes, layer cakes, tarts, and other luscious desserts are displayed on 3-tiered carts and rolled to your table for selection. This serving method can be copied for home entertaining, either by using a rolling cart or by displaying the desserts on a separate table.

SERVING SUGGESTIONS

There are actually three major methods of serving a meal—seated, buffet, and a combination of the two.

SEATED DINNER

Choose one from the following list:

1. Warmed plates are placed directly in front of the host. Immediately back of the plates is the roast with carving equipment. The host places the meat on the plate and the plate is passed to the hostess who serves the vegetables. The plate is then passed to the female guest of honor on the host's right; and so it goes until all are served. A method which cuts down on excessive passing is to have a helper or two carry each plate directly from host to hostess for the vegetables, then directly to the guest of honor. Follow this procedure until all are served.

2. The meat is carved in the kitchen and placed on warm plates along with the vegetables. Guests are called to dinner and when seated, a filled plate is placed in front of each.
3. When serving "family-style," the meat is placed on a platter in the kitchen, vegetables are ladled into serving dishes, rolls are placed in a basket in a napkin. Food, in various containers, is passed from one to another, starting with guest of honor, if any.
4. The most formal method of serving requires the services of a maid. Actually, it is similar to "family-style," in that food is placed in serving dishes. The maid brings in one item of food at a time (usually the meat first) and offers it to each guest, starting with the guest of honor and proceeding to the right around the table. She repeats this performance with the other items of food.

This method seems impractical to me unless you have one maid for each 4 people so that all food can be served in rapid succession before it gets cold.

TIPS FOR SETTING UP SEATED MEALS

There are several good reasons for seating guests at tables. The diners are more comfortable, conversation flows more easily, and there is less chance of awkward accidents. Men, especially, dislike balancing a plate on their knees. Here are several ways to increase seating space when you plan on serving a seated meal:

· Have the hardware store cut a 48- to 50-inch table top out of medium heavy plywood. A round shape is fine, but octagonal is better. This can be placed over a card table, thereby increasing your seating capacity from 4 to 8 people. A bonus advantage is that you have plenty of space for flowers and candles in the center.

· For outdoor parties, don't forget the system used by our grandparents. Three sawhorses were set up at equal distances and long planks were set over them. When they were covered with white tablecloths, who knew the difference?

· Think about the possibilities of a discarded door! Table legs are available in all shapes and heights and are easy to attach. Look in mail order catalogues or in a local building materials department. For a luau or Oriental feast, you might consider the shorter legs so that guests could sit on floor cushions.

· When entertaining in a small apartment, consider placing 2 card tables together and covering them with a single long tablecloth so that 6 people may sit together.

· A ping pong table is great for serving a lot of people. These tables measure 5 x 9 feet, and will accommodate 12 to 14 people.

· A poker table, with top cut to fit, is a grand help. The octagonal top will take care of 8 people.

· Don't overlook kitchen counter bars, family room game tables, let-down dining room shelves. All of these can be put to good use when having a large party.

· Banquet-sized tables are hard to work with, being long and usually narrow. Instead of placing them end to end as is customary, try placing them side by side. Two tables, each measuring $2\frac{1}{2}$ x 8 feet used in this manner will accommodate 12 to 14 people in comfort. The main advantage is that all will be able to participate in the same conversation, instead of being limited to the persons sitting on either side or across from you.

BUFFET SUPPERS

Buffet suppers have a way of being delightfully informal and can certainly put the hostess at ease. When space is limited such as in small apartments, meals are best managed in this way. Below are some of the methods used:

1. Food is placed in serving dishes on a table, shelf, or any flat surface—usually on top of a tablecloth or mats to protect the furniture. Guests serve themselves and sit where they choose.

2. Food is placed on a long, narrow table. At one end is a stack of lap trays. Hostess and a helper serve guests as they file by, which speeds up service. Trays are of course much more stable than just a plate on the lap.

3. Standing trays are very practical. Food is placed on the tray

in the kitchen, then brought out to each seated guest. This, of course, eliminates setting a buffet table, a boon if you have limited space. After everyone is finished, trays are whisked back to kitchen, leaving the living room as neat as before.

When chairs are at a minimum, brightly colored floor cushions are a practical substitute and can be luxurious. Most young people seem to enjoy sitting on the floor anyway—by the hearth, on the stairs, or in a cozy corner. People should be free to move around from one group to another.

SERVING BUFFET SUPPERS

The following technique will avoid that long line of guests waiting to serve themselves from the buffet table:

1. Set individual salads at each place at the set dining table.
2. Place all food on a separate table in the dining room, hot food in "bake-and-serve" casseroles or electric hot trays. Keep rolls hot in an electric bun warmer; preheated plates are stacked nearby.
3. Invite guests to come to the dining room and find their places at table. When all are seated, hostess takes her place.
4. Hostess starts eating her salad, thereby giving a signal for the rest to follow. She then makes an informal announcement something like this: "Some people prefer salad before the main course, some with it. When you are ready, will you please serve yourself?" One or two guests at a time leave the table to serve themselves and it is all done without confusion. Most important, the hostess is able to remain in the dining room most of the time.
5. Arrange in advance to have a close friend or relative help remove the used dishes when all have finished. Salts, peppers, and condiments should also be removed before dessert is served.

COMBINATION BUFFET-SEATED-SUPPER METHODS

1. A favorite method, which is a combination of the preceding ones, is to arrange the food on a buffet or side table. Have the

guests serve themselves, then find their places at the fully set dining table. If it is a large party, additional tables can be set up in the living room, family room, or sun porch. A hutch cabinet in the dining room lends itself well to this arrangement. The stack of warmed plates, the entrée, and vegetables can be placed on lower shelf, cups and saucers on the second shelf, and individual desserts on the top shelf. This makes it easy to serve dessert and coffee after the main course is finished.

2. Guests serve themselves from the dining tables, on which there are napkins and silverware as well as food. Guests sit at card tables which have only cloths on them. The advantage of this system is that if there is a space problem, you can set up the card tables at the last minute.

TIPS FOR INFORMAL PARTIES

· For very informal parties either seated or buffet, put a serving cart to work. Arrange individual plates of dessert on top shelf of cart. Remove used plates and put them on one of the lower shelves of cart, then serve the dessert before going on to the next guest.

· When you have several tables of guests, it's better to seat husbands and wives at the same table, though not necessarily next to one another. Conversation usually flows more naturally and in a more interesting way. As an example, let us say that the husband is a talented raconteur. It is likely that the wife will remind him of interesting experiences and stories which the other guests will enjoy. A knowledgeable conversationalist, however, will draw the remainder of the company out so that all may have an opportunity to take part and express opinions. Remember, the word ''conversation'' is defined as ''talking together—a verbal *exchange* of ideas and information.''

· It's a good idea to use place cards for any number of guests over 6. Make them out in advance to save confusion at the last moment. If you live near a gift shop or stationery store you'll have a selection of place cards from which to choose. However, acceptable ones can be cut from heavy stationery, 3- x 5-inch unlined cards, or notepaper. Simply cut paper into 3-inch squares, fold in two so that they will stand, and write the names.

"WHAT CAN I DO TO HELP?"

Sometimes the hostess would rather not have guests in the kitchen. On the other hand, an extra pair of hands can be very welcome.

The hostess can make serving a lot easier on herself if, in advance, she writes down the steps necessary in getting the meal served smoothly.

My method is a little sneaky, but it works!

Early in the day I cut slips of paper about 1 x 6 inches. As I think of ways in which I'll need help, I jot them down. As the girls arrive, fan them out and invite each to take one as if you are getting ready for a party game. Guests are delighted to help, and oh what a boon for the hostess.

Here are some samples:

Please pour one round of coffee.
Please light candles.
Please empty ashtrays when necessary.
Please help set dinner on table.
Please help serve dessert.

This will give you the idea. You take it from there.

SERVING DRINKS

Here are a few suggestions from which to choose:

If the host has a built-in bar in the den or family room, it is fairly easy to serve from there as he'll have all equipment at hand. Otherwise, all of the ingredients should be placed on a table or shelf or other flat surface which has been covered with first a plastic cloth, then a cotton or linen one. A 3-shelf rolling cart also works very well. The main consideration is to avoid making drinks in the kitchen while the hostess is busy with meal preparations.

If you plan on offering guests a wide selection of drinks, it's wise to engage a bartender if at all feasible. Otherwise, the host is kept constantly busy and has no time to circulate among the guests.

If using a serving table, you will find it convenient to have these things at hand: Bourbon, Scotch, Gin, appropriate mixes for each, 4-oz. cocktail glasses, 6-oz. old-fashioned glasses, 6- or 8-oz. glasses for mixed drinks. Always have tomato juice or nonalcoholic fruit punch available.

Other equipment needed: ice bucket filled with ice, long bar spoon, bar towel, measuring jiggers, cocktail picks, bottle openers, rubber tops, cocktail napkins.

For cocktails you'll need these garnishes: maraschino cherries, cocktail onions, lemon twists, lime slices, orange slices, stuffed olives.

An idea which works well for very informal parties, is to have a long sign made up at a shop which reads SELF SERVICE BAR. (It measures about 5 x 24 inches.) Display it where everyone can see it. Usually the host makes the first drink then invites people to replenish their own.

For very large receptions and parties, the punch bowl is the answer. Place 2 or 3 of them in various spots and guests serve themselves. All you need in each location is the bowl of punch on a tray, punch cups, a ladle, and cocktail napkins.

Sometimes waiters circulate through the rooms with trays of filled punch cups. This is done more often at weddings or other formal occasions.

PARTY PROPS

When you first start entertaining, you'll no doubt have to borrow or rent some of the necessary ''props,'' but as time goes on, you'll find it more convenient to own your own.

Here are some which you'll find very helpful:

Large punch bowl and ladle
30-cup coffee maker
Large bake-and-serve casseroles
Chafing dish
Extra large salad bowl and tongs

Large, compartmented serving dish (for choice of cocktail snack dips, relishes, toppings)

Electric hot trays

Snack trays, sometimes called lap trays, measuring 8½ x 14 inches with paper inserts. (These have depressions for plate, salad bowl, and cup or mug. They are indispensable when serving buffet-style.)

Folding snack tables or T.V. trays

STORING PARTY EQUIPMENT

Having the proper equipment is a big help in entertaining. The main problem, however, is storage, as some of these accessories, such as large salad bowls, large roasters, etc., are only used when you're having company.

A practical solution is to put your garage or basement to work. It is a comparatively simple task to build shelves and/or cupboards between the beams to store all those accessories and equipment which are used only a few times during the year.

Those heavy beams up high are great for hanging articles like Christmas decorations, wreaths, strings of Christmas lights, lightweight candelabra, wicker baskets, children's costumes, etc. I find that heavyweight florist wire comes in handy. (The brand I use is called Twist 'n Tye and comes in a can with a hole in the top.) In addition, save all those plastic bags from the cleaners. Measure a foot or two of wire, then double that again for extra strength. Slip the wire through a loop or handle on the article. Give it a twist or two, then slip a plastic bag over the article, bringing the wire out through the hole in the top of the bag. Make a knot in the bag below the article. (In this way, it is clearly visible and will remain clean between parties.) Slip the wire loop over one of the cup hooks which you have installed at regular distances along one of the heavy beams.

Your fine china, glassware, flat silver, and serving dishes are used primarily when you entertain. If stacked away in cupboards between parties, they usually need rewashing and polishing. To avoid this extra work, make use of the plastic, see-through bags which come in various sizes, in convenient rolls at a modest price.

China—after washing, let dry thoroughly. Place each type in a bag. Use a tie-twist to close bag. Place dinner plates in one, salad plates in another, saucers in another. Cups are safer wrapped singly, each in a sandwich size bag.

Glassware—wrap each glass separately. Secure top with rubber band.

Flat Silver—place all dinner knives in one bag, dinner forks in another, salad forks in another, and so on with the various pieces. Twist tie to close.

Serving Dishes—place dish in one bag and the cover in another. Twist tie to close. Place the top upside down on the serving dish so that you can stack another serving dish on top to conserve space.

CATERING SERVICES

When planning a large party such as a wedding reception, anniversary celebration, or other important function, it is often wise to engage the services of a catering company. In the long run, the cost is surprisingly low and the peace of mind is invaluable.

Here are some of the things a well-qualified catering service will do:

They supply tableware, cloths, napkins, serving dishes, punchbowls and cups, and they will set the tables. They supply all the food, bringing it all prepared and in suitable containers from which to serve. If you wish, they will supply the beverages, even the wedding cake. They will bring waiters, bartender if necessary, and man to park cars.

They straighten up afterward, removing food and tables as quickly as possible after the meal is finished. Your kitchen should be left in immaculate condition.

Catering services vary tremendously of course in different parts of the country, especially in regard to the amount charged. Depending on the menu served, the number of guests, the amount of help needed, a certain amount is charged per person.

I have listed some of the things the caterer does. Now, there are certain things that you must do.

The most important thing to remember is that for your protection and the caterer's, every point about the menu and the serving must be mutually understood. The only safe and satisfactory method is to have it all down in writing. Most catering firms have order forms and the customer gets a copy. Make sure that the price quoted includes tax and tips.

To avoid disappointment, contact your caterer well in advance to set the date. Have a personal conference with him as to your menu and all other details.

Advise him several days in advance as to firm guest count.

Most catering companies have specialties which they prepare exceptionally well. They usually prefer to serve foods that they've served before. However, some companies will prepare anything the hostess stipulates.

In smaller communities where there is no catering service, you may be able to secure the services of an individual cateress. You plan the menu, shop for supplies, and she prepares the food in your own kitchen, possibly bringing someone to help her with the cooking and serving.

SETTING THE SCENE

FLOWER ARRANGEMENTS AND PARTY CENTERPIECES

Fresh flowers, tastefully arranged, add charm and beauty to a home. When planning your garden, plant flowers in colors which are harmonious with the colors in your rooms.

A dark-paneled room usually cries out for white. The following varieties are possible choices:

Spring—white camellias, iris, stock, pansies, tulips and hyacinths
Summer—white roses, gardenias, daisies, petunias, carnations
Autumn—white asters, chrysanthemums, variegated green and
  white ivy

Winter—consider using dish gardens of green plants with two or three fresh white flowers from the florist tucked here and there

For a white, pale pink or blue room, you can use all the pastels —pink begonias, lavender ageratum, pale blue pansies and Dutch iris, double pink petunias, cascading pink and orchid fuschias.

Fresh flowers in the kitchen, particularly over the sink, can brighten up the dullest day. For a white or yellow kitchen use white daisies, yellow and white narcissuses, yellow chrysanthemums.

FLOWERING PLANTS Flowering plants brighten up the house for winter entertaining. They pay big dividends, particularly in mild climates, as they can be planted in the garden after they have finished blooming indoors and live to bloom another day.

In the fall plant bulbs in pretty ceramic, metal or china flower pots. You'll be enchanted when they break into gorgeous bloom in early spring in a sunny window. Particularly lovely are narcissuses, tulips, and daffodils.

Don't overlook the beauty of trailing and blooming house plants such as ivy, philodendron, African violets, angel-wing begonias, etc.

FLORAL CENTERPIECES Decorations for your party table are called centerpieces no matter where they are placed on the table. Remember to arrange centerpieces low so that guests can easily see over them. Here are some ideas:

- Use a pair of flower arrangements, one at each side of a single candelabrum.
- Place three long, narrow containers filled with short-stemmed flowers close together to make an unbroken line of flowers. Candles are set at each end. Guests are seated only at sides of table.
- Select flowers which will enhance the overall effect of your table setting. As an example, pink and white roses in a silver bowl would be very pretty with rose-sprigged china; bold zinnias or marigolds would be fetching with peasant-type pottery in earthy colors.

· Watch that flowers do not cascade into salads, butter plates, or goblets.

PAPER PARTY GOODS

Take advantage of all the beautiful colorful paper goods now available. Stores carry complete lines of coordinated goods in different themes for children's parties—invitations, paper table-cloths, napkins, plates, cups, centerpieces.

For adult parties, paper plates which fit into wicker containers and compartmented paper liners, designed to fit into small metal trays are indispensable, particularly for lap eating.

Cocktail napkins, dinner napkins in rich, solid colors, place mats, coasters, and guest towels are all time-savers, not only for parties, but for daily use.

Paper goods may be combined with your own china, silver, and linen.

As an example, you could use a forest green linen cloth on your table. On top of that use colorful floral paper place mats with napkins to match. Paper coasters in the same design will be pretty under the goblets and protect your table. To save space use a miniature bouquet of fresh flowers on a small paper lace doily in front of each place setting, instead of a large bouquet in the center. Containers can be after-dinner cups and saucers, liqueur, or wine glasses or even baby food jars with ivy or fern or other greens to disguise the rims. You need only three or four fresh posies for it to be effective.

You can now buy rolls of paper designed for table coverings for club banquets and church affairs. These are in a variety of colors, about 42″ wide and are perforated at intervals so that you can tear off the lengths you need. For outdoor parties, it's best to make a double fold at each corner and thumbtack it to the picnic table.

Plastic knives, forks, and spoons are now available in a variety of colors for pennies. The newer ones are so sturdy that they can easily be used for steak or chicken. To make cutting easier, the knives are serrated. They're widely available in supermarkets and party goods shops and in my opinion, are the only thing for outdoor parties.

ENTERTAINMENT

CONVERSATION

Samuel Johnson used the phrase, ''the excellencies of lively conversation.'' Stimulating conversation is, and always has been, the finest entertainment known to man. Nowhere do we need it more than at a party. When your guests are good conversationalists you need no other entertainment.

One of the most important assets in becoming an accomplished host or hostess is the ability to direct conversation into interesting channels which are of interest to all.

The art of good conversation can be acquired. Here's one way to start: When you read the newspaper or a magazine or go to a lecture, keep a notebook handy. Each time you read or hear something which is newsworthy, interesting, or provocative, jot down a word or two as a reminder. For each hour of reading you'll probably find ten to twelve topics of general interest. A few that come to mind are travel, medical discoveries, housing innovations, gardening, outer space projects, plays and movies, television programs, celebrities, Dear Abby problems, storms, pets, scenic points of interest, accidents, the occult, etc.

These topics are not of interest to all people nor are they profound, but the majority of people are interested in them.

Keep adding to your list of topics and stories every day if possible. Prop it up on your dresser where you can refer to it often. Next time you're at a party or other gathering, you'll be surprised how much you are able to contribute to the conversation. You'll also discover how much more you will enjoy other people's, if you really listen to what they have to say. Try it— you'll see!

MUSIC

Music plays a surprisingly important part in entertaining. Our spirits soar the moment we hear a familiar, lively tune and we know from the start that it's going to be a wonderful party.

Live music is, of course, ideal and, in many cases, surprisingly inexpensive. Among your own friends there are usually several people who enjoy playing, whether it be piano, guitar, or accordion. In the absence of live music don't overlook stereo record players and tape recorders. There are many wonderful records and tapes available where you can sing along with the musicians. Singalongs are as enjoyable now as they were in Grandmother's day.

Active participation, such as the Tin Pan Band, otherwise known as The Kitchen Band is great fun for everyone from 3 to 93. (See Fourth of July Family Reunion.)

Music has been called "the universal language" and when giving a special party with a theme, you can easily create atmosphere with appropriate music. See suggestions for music in the various parties in this book.

GAMES FOR ADULTS

Games and contests, when chosen wisely, add tremendously to the enjoyment of a party, especially those celebrating such occasions as St. Patrick's Day, Valentine's Day, New Year's Eve, Halloween, or ones with a Wild West theme, Hill Billy Hoedown, Hobo theme, Stork Shower, etc.

The failure or success of party games depends a great deal on the way they are presented by the hostess. If she half-heartedly says, "Now who would like to play games?" she might expect groans and head shaking. On the other hand if she says, "I have a great game and lots of prizes. I'm sure you'll enjoy it. Here's how it's played," she can usually expect enthusiasm and an upbeat, almost instantly, in the tempo of the party.

Don't hesitate about including games for a mixed party. Men

are very adept at games, particularly Charades and contests where men are on one team and women on the other.

It's better to avoid quizzes and other intellectual games. There's no doubt that some people shine at them, but too often there are others who don't, and this becomes embarrassing to all.

You'll find a good selection of treasure hunts, relays and party games in the individual parties in the book.

GAMES FOR CHILDREN

When organizing for family reunions or other occasions where children are included, it is necessary to make provision for their entertainment. Things go much smoother if there is an adult or teenager in attendance to explain and referee the games.

There are several things which are very easy to do that don't require much advance planning. One that is great is the Wall Mural. Buy the widest white shelf paper available and either staple or tack it on a fence, side of a garage, a patio floor, or any flat surface. If possible, extend it about 15 feet. With a felt marking pen, divide it into sections so that each child will have a space in which to paint. Have a good supply of crayons or finger paints in vivid colors. One method which works very well is to give them categories. You might say, "Let's see—who can draw the most beautiful house? or the prettiest flower? or the most savage wild animal?"

An alternate way would be to say, "Now we're going to draw a city street with houses, stores, chimneys, clouds, people, dogs, birds, etc. Let's see what a beautiful wall mural you can paint in half an hour." Other murals could be A Pet Contest; Jungleland; The Circus; A Beautiful Garden; Halloween Night.

This will keep them happy, they'll try very hard, it's inventive, and everyone will get a great deal of pleasure out of viewing the final results.

Family parties are happy parties, particularly when games are planned as part of the entertainment.

See parties for Mother's Day, Father's Day, Easter, Fourth of July, and other special holidays.

One of the best icebreakers is a hunt of some kind.

A penny hunt, preferably outdoors, will keep them occupied for 15 or 20 minutes. Hide them on window ledges, a garden walk, on a tree trunk, or tape them to garden tools. Paint one red. Whoever finds that gets 25¢.

Instead of pennies, you can use peanuts in the shell. Give each one a little sack in which to gather them.

Gummed seals are excellent for hunts and are available in many patterns for special occasions. There are usually 6 designs on a page, 30 seals in a package. You can get them for St. Patrick's Day, Easter, Christmas, Halloween, Thanksgiving. There are also flowers, birds, and animals.

When using seals, it is best to stick just a small section to the surface so that the child can easily remove it. Here again it's a good idea to give each a small sack in which to bring back his seals. Award a small prize for the most productive hunter.

GAMES AND CONTESTS—STORAGE A cupboard or drawer reserved for game equipment is worth its weight in gold. Keep on hand playing cards and scoring tablets; poker chips; a dart game set of good quality, dice and a shaker; Bingo set; miscellaneous games for children such as Snakes and Ladders, Old Maid, Chinese Checkers, Anagrams; song books or song sheets.

PARTY RECORD

Be sure to keep a record of your parties, not only to avoid serving the same menu to the same guests, but to be able to give the same party for a different group of guests with very little effort. Once you have the party planned, the menu and shopping lists made out, your method of serving planned and schedules made out, it is comparatively easy to stage a repeat performance.

This also enables you to make corrections in your planning, such as allowing more time for flower arranging, setting the table, or whatever.

Here, too, you can make note of guests' food preferences, such as "No sweets for Mary," "Joe can't bear fish," or "Harvey loves chocolate cake."

Spring
Parties

- 🎏 *MARCH*
- 🌷 *APRIL*
- 🎐 *MAY*

St. Patrick's Day Supper

FOR 8

7:00 to 10:00 P.M.

Health and long life to you
Land without rent to you
A child every year to you
And may you die in Ireland.
  (OLD IRISH TOAST)

St. Patrick's Day, March 17, has been observed in the United States since the eighteenth century. The most spectacular celebration is the annual St. Patrick's Day parade in New York City. This special day is also celebrated extensively at club and church affairs and at parties in private homes.

Get the party off to a good start by sending written invitations. If they are cleverly worded, they give promise of fun in store and create happy anticipation for guests.

Oh come all you Kellys, O'Rourkes, and Deneen,
Tuck under your arm your fav'rite colleen.
We've a cellar well stored
And a plentiful board.
Now don't you forget to be wearin' the green.

If your Irish luck is with you, you'll find green-bordered note paper; otherwise, decorate by using a shamrock seal at the top.

MENU

For this informal party we're suggesting a menu made up mostly of finger foods.

*Spareribs in "Open Pit" Barbecue Sauce
French Fried Potatoes
*Marinated Fresh Vegetables
*Irish Soda Bread
*Leprechaun Dessert Mold   *Shamrock Cookies
*Irish Coffee

RECIPES

SPARERIBS IN
"OPEN PIT" BARBECUE SAUCE

2 ingredients

SERVES: 8

Equipment: large roasting pan

6 pounds spareribs*
1 28-ounce bottle barbecue sauce (I use Good Seasons' Open Pit Barbecue Sauce.)

*Select lean, meaty, fresh pork ribs which are pink in color. Have the butcher chop through ribs at large end. Sometimes he will also cut them into serving pieces.

Method:
1. Cut sheets of spareribs into serving portions of 2 or 3 ribs each.
2. Place in roasting pan and bake in 325° oven for 45 minutes.
3. Pour excess grease from spareribs. Cover with sauce.
4. Bake an additional 45 minutes or until fork-tender and rich brown in color. Don't overcook.

MARINATED FRESH VEGETABLES

4 ingredients

YIELD : approximately 4 cups

1 medium head cauliflower
6–8 carrots (new spring carrots if possible)
2 medium-sized turnips*
1 8-ounce bottle oil and vinegar salad dressing (I use Kraft.)

*Add or substitute any crisp vegetable of your choice—radishes, zucchini, scallions, green peppers, celery.

Method:
1. Clean vegetables carefully. Separate cauliflower into individual "florets," and cut other vegetables thinly, on the diagonal, but large enough to be eaten with fingers.
2. Marinate vegetables in salad dressing in coldest part of refrigerator for several hours before serving time.
3. Pour into bowl, dressing and all.

Note: Makes a good finger food for cocktail parties or informal suppers in place of salad.

IRISH SODA BREAD

4 ingredients

YIELD : 1 medium-sized loaf

Equipment: loaf pan or pie plate

1 teaspoon baking soda
1 cup seedless raisins
2 cups buttermilk
4 cups self-rising flour

Method:
1. Add baking soda and raisins to buttermilk in a large bowl.
2. Stir flour into buttermilk mixture and stir until dough leaves sides of bowl. Transfer to a greased pie plate or loaf pan.
3. Cut a deep cross in top of dough. The cross is characteristic of Irish Soda Bread.
4. Bake 45 minutes in 375° oven until light brown, or until toothpick comes out clean.

Note: Makes wonderful toast, or you can slice bread thin, butter generously, and reheat in oven.

LEPRECHAUN DESSERT MOLD

4 ingredients

SERVES: 8

Equipment: 2-quart mold, or parfait or sherbet dishes

 2 envelopes unflavored gelatin
5–6 medium eggs, separated
1½ cups green crème de menthe liqueur
 1 pint heavy cream for whipping

Method:
1. Mix gelatin with 1 cup cold water in saucepan.
2. Add egg yolks and stir until thoroughly blended.
3. Place over low heat and stir constantly until gelatin dissolves and mixture thickens slightly (about 5 minutes).
4. Remove from heat and stir in crème de menthe.
5. Chill, stirring occasionally, until mixture mounds slightly when dropped from spoon.
6. Beat egg whites until very stiff. Fold into gelatin mixture.
7. Whip the cream and fold into mixture.
8. Turn into 2-quart mold or into parfait or sherbet glasses. Chill several hours or overnight.

SHAMROCK COOKIES

4 ingredients

YIELD : 18

Equipment: cookie sheet; 3-inch shamrock or 1-inch heart cookie cutter

½ cup sugar
½ pound butter or margarine
3 cups self-rising flour
1 can green decorator frosting

Method:
1. Beat together the sugar, softened butter, and 2 tablespoons water. I use an electric beater.
2. Add flour gradually until well blended, then knead for a few moments until pliable, as if you were making piecrust.
3. Roll small amounts of dough, ¼-inch thick, on a lightly floured board. Cut with shamrock cookie cutter. If you don't have a shamrock cuttter, place 3 1-inch heart-shaped cookies together on a plate and add a stem made by rolling dough between hands to the size of a cigarette, then shaping into a half circle.
4. Bake on ungreased cookie sheet 10–12 minutes at 350°, until light brown in color.
5. Pipe around the edge of each cookie with green decorator frosting.

IRISH COFFEE

4 ingredients

SERVES : 8

Equipment: Irish Coffee glasses, large wine glasses, or tall hot-chocolate cups

1 cup heavy cream for whipping
$\frac{1}{4}$ cup granulated sugar
$1\frac{1}{3}$ cups Irish whiskey
6 cups strong black coffee, piping hot

Method:
1. Whip the cream until it forms soft peaks.
2. Place 2 teaspoons sugar in each of 8 Irish Coffee glasses.
3. Add 2 tablespoons Irish whiskey to each glass.
4. Fill glass with coffee to within an inch of the top. Stir.
5. Top with a rounded tablespoon of whipped cream, or to taste.

Note: Do not stir. Sip the delightful concoction through the whipped cream topping.

TIPS FOR PREPARING AND SERVING Serve family style. Place food in platters and serving dishes and pass from one to another at table.

Arrange half the Barbecued Spareribs on one platter, half on another and place a platter at each end of table. Serve very hot!

Heap the French Fries into two vegetable dishes and place one at each end of table. Serve hot!

Pass the Marinated Fresh Vegetables in a large bowl. Serve icy cold!

Several hours beforehand, cut the Irish Soda Bread into slices, toast and butter, and wrap tightly in foil. Heat in oven just before supper. Lay foil-wrapped bread in basket and pass at table. Serve hot.

At the end of the main course, remove dishes and napkins to kitchen. Supply fresh napkins for dessert.

Serve Leprechaun Dessert Mold in parfait or sherbet glasses, icy cold.

Arrange Shamrock Cookies on a plate. Pass at table. Serve at room temperature.

Make Irish Coffee in kitchen or set ingredients and cups or glasses on tray and prepare in front of guests. Set cup at right of each guest.

SETTING THE SCENE

PADDY PIG TABLE SETTING   To cover a 72-inch table, buy 2½–3 yards of white oilcloth, 42 inches wide, usually available at a ten-cent store. With pinking shears, cut around edge of material or, if you like, cut the edges into scallops.

For place mats, draw a pig on a piece of heavyweight construction paper 12 x 18 inches. Use this as a pattern. Lay pattern on green oilcloth and trace with a felt pen. Cut with pinking shears.

Use Kelly green and white paper napkins folded together so that both colors show, or use bibs. Draw a bib on a piece of art paper 12 x 18 inches. Use this as a pattern. Lay pattern on green oilcloth and trace with a felt pen. Cut with pinking shears or sharp scissors. Staple two pieces of ribbon about 24 inches long at the shoulders for ties.

Use oval white paper plates.

The materials for your centerpiece include a pair of inexpensive green top hats, available at a variety store or party shop. Punch holes in top of crown. Stick fresh daffodils or narcissus through holes into a bowl of water under each hat.

To hold your candles, use scrubbed medium-sized potatoes. Lay each lengthwise. In center make a hole with an apple corer. Insert long Kelly green candles. Should potatoes wobble, cut a thin slice from bottom side so that candles will stand upright. To protect your table, place a small square of foil under the potatoes.

Place cards should be plain white with a shamrock sticker on each. Cards read: Mrs. O'Smith, Mr. O'Brent, Miss O'Barnes, Mrs. O'Perez, Mr. O'McCroskey, etc.

Hallmark has a booklet of very fetching shamrock, leprechaun, and harp seals. They are inexpensive and can be used on place cards, invitations, etc.

Set white clay pipe and a small pouch of tobacco at each place. An alternate idea is to present each girl with a green hairbow and each man with a green bow tie.

ENTERTAINMENT

SINGALONG   None can lift up his voice in song like an Irishman, so don't overlook any of these:

> "Peggy O'Neil"
> "My Wild Irish Rose"
> "When Irish Eyes Are Smiling"
> "Peg O' My Heart"
> "It's Only a Shanty in Old Shanty Town"
> "A Little Bit of Heaven"
> "Little Annie Rooney"
> "Danny Boy"
> "I'll Take You Home Again, Kathleen"
> "McNamara's Band"
> "Mother Machree"
> "Cockles and Mussels"
> "Toora Loora Loora"
> "The Wearin' of the Green"
> "It's a Long Way to Tipperary"

Supper Shower
for the Bride and Groom

FOR 16

Sunday, 4 :00 to 8 :00 P.M.

For a newly married couple just moving into their first home, a garden shower is one of the most practical and satisfying of all parties. From the viewpoint of the young couple, there are so many other expenses that often there is nothing left for landscaping. From the viewpoint of friends attending the shower, it is gratifying to know that their plant gifts are living ones, becoming larger and more beautiful as time goes by.

Shopping is easy for this type of shower, for a wide range of possible gifts is available. In addition to trees, shrubs, bulbs, potted plants, flats of flowering seedlings and packets of seeds, there is a wide selection of gardening tools such as a rake, hoe, spade, shovel, pick, flower shears, trowels, garden hose, and sprinklers. Consider also hanging baskets, flower pots, and window boxes. Don't forget one of the most essential gifts of all—an easy, how-to book on gardening so that they'll know how to plant all the glorious gifts. Shady straw hats and gardening gloves are also welcome.

Wheel in the gifts in a garden cart.

I see this as a Sunday party with the schedule something like this :

        4 :00 P.M. : Guests arrive.
                     They are served punch and appetizers.
        5 :00 P.M. : Early supper is served.
        6 :00 P.M. : After-supper fun.
        7 :00 P.M. : Gifts are opened.
        8 :00 P.M. : ''Home Sweet Home.''

$\mathcal{M}ENU$

Planter's Punch
*"Nuts and Bolts" Nibblers
Garden Patch Salad
*Turkey Cottage Pie
Stuffed Mushrooms   Broiled Tomatoes
*Flower Pot Desserts
Tea   Coffee

$\mathcal{R}ECIPES$

"NUTS AND BOLTS" NIBBLERS

4 ingredients

YIELD: approximately 5 cups

Equipment: 9- x 13-inch baking pan

1 large, 16-ounce package rice or wheat cereal
1 cup salted nuts
1 tablespoon seasoned salt (or more to taste)
   (I use Lawry's.)
½ cup butter (1 stick)
   Optional: 1 6-ounce package pretzel sticks

Method:
1. Pour cereal, nuts, pretzels, if desired, and seasoned salt into large paper bag.
2. Dribble half the melted butter over the mixture. Shake well.
3. Pour mixture into 9- x 13-inch baking pan. Bake 30 minutes at 300°.
4. Pour mixture back into bag, drizzle remaining butter over it, and shake bag well.
5. Return to oven and continue baking 30 minutes longer. Remove from oven, stir, and let dry a little before storing.

TURKEY COTTAGE PIE

4 ingredients

SERVES: **16**

Equipment: 2 9- x 13-inch baking dishes

- 4 packages frozen mixed vegetables (I use Birdseye Parisian.)
- 8 cups cooked turkey chunks, approximately 1 inch*
- 4 cans condensed cream of chicken soup (I use Campbell's.)
- 4 cups mashed potatoes (Leftovers are fine.)

*Very practical for this dish is boned rolled turkey, widely available now in frozen foods departments. (I use Checkerboard brand.)

Method:

1. Prepare vegetables according to directions on package. Pour cooked vegetables into 2 buttered 9- x 13-inch baking dishes.
2. Arrange 4 cups of cooked turkey chunks over the vegetables in each dish.
3. Mix 4 cans soup with 2 cans water, then pour half over each turkey-vegetable mixture.
4. Spoon 2 cups mashed potatoes over each casserole. Fluff up with fork.
5. Bake at 450° for 12–15 minutes or until potatoes have brown peaks and mixture is bubbling.

FLOWER POT DESSERTS

One of the prettiest and most delicious desserts I've ever run into are these colorful tempters. Eight small clay pots on a tray, with fresh roses blooming luxuriously, are a gay sight indeed and many will be the compliments you receive when you serve them. Best of all, they are no trouble to make and may be assembled far in advance. Remove from freezing compartment just before serving time. (You may want to paint the little pots to harmonize with your china. An easy way is to invert them over a milk bottle and turn the bottle as you paint or spray.)
You will need:

> 8 red clay flower pots, about 4 inches deep
> 2 packages ladyfingers
> 1 ½ quarts peppermint-stick ice cream
> 1 square grated chocolate
> 8 fresh rosebuds
> Aluminum foil

Wash pots thoroughly in hot water and soap, then dip into boiling water to sterilize. Dry carefully. Line each with halves of ladyfingers. Fill pot with ice cream. Grate chocolate over the top. Wrap each in aluminum foil. Freeze until ready to serve.

Stems of roses should be about 5 inches long. Wrap stems tightly in foil. When ready to serve, pierce the ice cream with an ice pick and insert the rose stem in the hole. When all are finished, place flower pot desserts on a tray and pass.

TIPS FOR PREPARING AND SERVING Make up recipe for Planter's Punch in large glass pitcher. At serving time, place pitcher in punch bowl, then pour crushed ice around the pitcher. Let stand for a few minutes before using. It will make a nice hollow spot so that you can replace pitcher after pouring drinks. Have garnishes at hand and replace when necessary.

Pour "Nuts and Bolts" into several bowls. Place on tables for leisurely munching with drinks.

Prepare Garden Patch Salad in two bowls. Place one on each side of buffet table for duplicate service.

Make two Turkey Cottage Pies. Place one on each side of buffet table.

Place Stuffed Mushrooms on two platters or bake-and-serve dishes.

Handle Broiled Tomatoes same as mushrooms.

Remove Flower Pot Desserts from freezer 10–15 minutes before serving. Stick rose in each. Place all on tray and serve after main-course dishes are removed.

It is pleasant to have drinks and supper outdoors on a patio or under a spreading shade tree.

Lawn furniture, arranged in conversational groups, might be augmented with folding chairs as needed. Standing trays are the ideal solution for a buffet supper. If you don't have enough for all, fill in with regular trays. The main point is to provide guests with a stable surface from which to eat and a place to set a coffee cup.

Even though we plan on eating outdoors, I usually place the food on the dining table, which is near the kitchen. It saves a great many steps for the hostess, and the food stays hot or cold.

Invite guests to serve themselves, then find a spot in the garden.

SETTING THE SCENE

Either use a solid-color tablecloth with printed paper napkins to harmonize, or a flowered print cloth with napkins in a solid color.

The plates, either paper or plastic, could be the divided type— spaces for food and a separate compartment for cup or glass. Set each in its matching tray and make a stack at one end of table.

Hot drink paper cups could be arranged around a large, 30-cup coffeemaker at opposite end of table.

A very fetching and appropriate centerpiece could be made by arranging toy watering cans filled with fresh flowers, flanked by toy garden implements, such as a rake and hoe, propped up nearby.

Another idea is to spray a watering can to match your color scheme, fill it with fresh flowers and cascading vines, and suspend from chandelier or ceiling over your buffet table. Narrow, clear cellophane streamers, such as those used to decorate Christmas trees, can be attached to spout to resemble water.

ENTERTAINMENT

CLOTHESPIN GAME   My charming neighbor plays this at their parties, and it is a riot. She collects about 75 spring-type clothespins and puts them in a bag with 2 handles. Partners, usually a man and woman, are blindfolded and each has a handle over the left wrist. At the word ''Go'' they start pinning clothespins on one another at a great rate—to lapels, collars, ties, ruffles, even hair. At the end of 60 seconds the bell rings, blindfolds are removed, and the total clothespins that they used are counted. Then the next couple goes through the same procedure. Give prizes to the couple who pinned the most.

''GROCERY LIST'' BEE—Do you remember how the old-fashioned spelling bees were conducted? Members of one team faced the members of the other. A word to spell was given to the first one in line on a team. Then a word was given to the first one in line on the opposing team. When a player missed, he was disqualified and the word went to the next in line on the opposing team. And so it went, back and forth, until all were disqualified except one, who, of course, won the prize.

This game follows this procedure except that the object is to make up a grocery list.

First player names a food. The first player on the opposite side has to name a food beginning with the last letter of the previous word. The list might go something like this: apple, eggs, soup, parsley, yeast, tea, almonds, starch, honey, yams, sugar, rice. At this point several might fall by the wayside, as there aren't too many groceries beginning with ''e.'' Of course a food must be mentioned only once. Harder than you'd think!

WHAT'S THE NAME OF THAT GADGET?   Here's a game for men only:

Before the party, assemble 15 or 20 hard-to-identify utensils. Mark each with a number (a self-stick seal or adhesive tape works fine). Keep them in a bag or drawer until game time.

Have ready for each player an entry form on which is written or typed:

> 1. . . . .
> 2. . . . .
> 3. . . . . etc.

(as many numbers as you have utensils)

Hand each of the men an entry form. Place all of the utensils or gadgets on a card table and call ''Ready, set, go!''

As the men are able to identify the various utensils, they mark in the name opposite. He who identifies the most items correctly wins the prize. Guess what? A chef's hat for barbecuing.

Here are a few items which may cause them trouble: colander; mortar and pestle; grapefruit knife; egg slicer; butter cube slicer; layer cake cutter; cork puller; egg separator; apple or pear slicer; tomato slicer; garlic press; omelet pan; lid opener; gelatin ring mold; angel cake pan—well, you get the idea.

WHAT'S THE NAME OF THIS FLOWER?   Here's an alternate game which is highly appropriate for a garden shower.

Before the party, cut out colored pictures of 25 or 30 flowers or flowering plants from flower catalogues, seed packets, or magazines. Most of them should be easily identifiable, but include a few puzzlers. Number each picture. Tack them up at intervals on a fence, or if that isn't practical, tack or tape them to a bulletin board or door or any large flat surface.

Give each guest an entry blank and pencil. At the word ''Go,'' they start writing the names of the flower opposite each number. First one to turn in a perfect score wins the prize.

The Business Couple
Gives a Sunday Brunch

11:00 A.M. to 2:00 P.M. or after church

Business couples are entertaining more than they did even ten short years ago. Men, as well as women, are becoming more interested in food preparations, especially when delicious concoctions can be whipped up with little effort.

Giving a Sunday or holiday brunch is great fun and a particularly pleasant way to entertain out-of-town guests, celebrate a special occasion, or give a bride-and-groom shower. One great advantage is that host, hostess, and guests alike are rested, relaxed, and unhurried, and men particularly seem to enjoy the companionship of friends and family at a Sunday brunch more than at any other form of entertaining.

The following party is planned as a seated meal for 8.

MENU

A brunch menu is ordinarily made up of a combination of breakfast and luncheon foods and should include a before-brunch drink, fruit, eggs, meat or fish, bread or rolls, and a beverage.

In planning your menu, think of items which may be prepared in advance so that all you have to do is to whisk them from the refrigerator or oven without a lot of nerve-shattering, last-minute tasks.

*Snappy Bloody Marys or Pitcher of Iced Tomato Juice
Sparkling Fruit in Champagne
*Mushroom-Egg Scallop on *Toast Points or in *Patty Shells
Oven-Browned Canadian Bacon Slices
*Miniature Mincemeat Coffee Cakes
Coffee

RECIPES

SNAPPY BLOODY MARYS

4 ingredients

YIELD : 1 quart (easier to make and store in quart batches)

Equipment: extra ice trays; 1-quart jar or pitcher

    2 10-ounce cans highly seasoned tomato cocktail (I use
      Snap-E-Tom.)
    Celery sticks (allow one for each drink)
    3 cups tomato juice
    ¾ cup vodka

Method:
1. Freeze seasoned tomato cocktails in ice trays for several hours
   or overnight. I make plenty of these ahead of time and store
   them in large Baggies in freezer compartment.
2. Clean the celery. Cut into pieces about 6 inches long and ½
   inch wide. Store in jar of water in refrigerator.
3. Combine tomato juice and vodka in quart jar. Cover. Store in
   refrigerator until serving time.
4. Put 3 or 4 tomato cocktail ice cubes in each glass. Pour in vodka–
   tomato juice mixture to fill glass.
5. Insert celery stick in each for stirrer.

Note: Gone are those watery Bloody Marys. These get better tast-
   ing every sip as the tomato cocktail cubes melt.

MUSHROOM-EGG SCALLOP

5 ingredients

SERVES : 8

Equipment : large casserole

8 eggs
1 pound fresh mushrooms
¼ pound butter
3 cans white sauce
8 slices toast, or 8 patty shells*

*See next page for recipes.

Method:
1. Hard boil the eggs. Rinse immediately in cold water.
2. Scrub mushrooms under running water with soft brush. Drain thoroughly. Wipe dry with paper towels. With sharp knife, slice through top and stem vertically.
3. Melt butter in large skillet. Cook mushrooms until slightly browned and soft. Set aside.
4. Pour cream sauce into the skillet and mix well with the remaining melted butter.
5. Slice each egg into 4 equal parts.
6. Fold eggs and mushrooms carefully into cream sauce.
7. Pour into large casserole and bake in preheated oven at 350° for 10–15 minutes, or until bubbling hot. Serve over toast points or in patty shells.

TOAST POINTS

3 ingredients

SERVES: 8

Equipment: large muffin tin

8 slices sandwich bread
¼ pound butter or margarine
½ teaspoon onion or garlic salt or mixed herbs (I use Lawry's brand called Pinch of Herbs.)

Method:
1. Cut crusts from bread.
2. Melt butter. Stir in onion or garlic salt or herbs.
3. Brush bread slices with melted butter.
4. Press slices into cups of large muffin tin.
5. Bake 10–12 minutes in 400° oven. Fill with Mushroom-Egg Scallop.

PATTY SHELLS

At last you can get patty shells, ready to be baked, in the frozen food section. (I use Pepperidge Farm.)

Bake the patty shells several hours before the party, for convenience. Reheat for a few minutes before filling; you'll find them unbelievably light and flaky. Follow directions carefully regarding oven temperature.

MINIATURE MINCEMEAT COFFEE CAKES

4 ingredients

YIELD : 20

Equipment: kitchen shears; cookie sheet; rolling pin

2 rolls refrigerator buttermilk biscuits
1 cup bottled mincemeat
1 cup brown sugar
1 cup chopped walnuts

Method:
1. Roll each unbaked biscuit out thin on a lightly floured board.
2. Spread each with about 1 teaspoon mincemeat and roll up like jelly roll, then shape in circle. Cut slits around edge of circle with kitchen shears.
3. Sprinkle each with about 1 teaspoon brown sugar and 1 teaspoon chopped nuts.
4. Bake at 350° for about 15 minutes until golden brown.

TIPS FOR PREPARING AND SERVING   Several hours ahead make Bloody Marys in a pitcher and/or a pitcher of Iced Tomato Juice. Chill in refrigerator. When guests arrive, set pitchers on a large tray with glasses and cocktail napkins and bowl of tomato cocktail ice cubes.

Chill the fruit and champagne separately. At serving time, spoon fruit into sherbet dishes and pour ⅓ cup champagne over each serving. Set on small plates. While guests are on first course, reheat the Mushroom-Egg Scallop and Toast Points or Patty Shells.

Brown the Canadian Bacon Slices and reheat Miniature Mincemeat Coffee Cakes at same time.

Make large pot of coffee well in advance.

SETTING THE SCENE

Brunch is usually set in a more informal manner than luncheon or dinner. You may use pottery dishes, bright colored tablecloth and napkins, wickerware baskets and wooden accessories. An air of relaxed informality should be your objective.

In the winter, when flowers are in short supply, I use individual Swedish bud vases, one in front of each plate. Two or three small flowers and a piece of green vine give a surprisingly pretty effect, especially on a round or oval table.

In the spring, I arrange a pyramid of eggs in a milkglass compote with posies tucked in the niches.

In summer, when the days are fine, we set up a large, round table in the garden in the shade of a large tree. A violet-sprigged tablecloth with linen napkins of royal purple is pretty against the green of leaf and lawn. To save space in the center of the table, I suspend my centerpiece from a convenient tree limb. It is a wicker bird cage which I fill with fresh flowers in a rainbow of colors. Small-leaf ivy cascades over the edges. It just clears the table.

In the autumn, I arrange a pyramid of red or golden Delicious apples in a footed wicker basket, with autumn leaves tucked in between. Sometimes I use a small wooden cart overflowing with small vegetables such as radishes, mushrooms, baby carrots, small white onions, dried red peppers, string beans, and shelled peas. You can tuck small sprigs of parsley into crevices.

Easter Lunch

1:00 to 3:30 P.M.

At no time in the year are spirits soaring higher, flowers blooming more brightly, birds singing more ecstatically. You couldn't possibly have a more wonderful atmosphere in which to get family and friends together.

MENU

*Spring Welcome Punch
*Nut-Coated Chicken Breasts   *Oriental Fruit Sauce
Fluffy Baked Rice
*Creamy Tomato Aspic Louis
Prebaked packaged rolls
*Daffodil Cake
Tea   Coffee
"Take home" treat for children:
*Homemade Chocolate Easter Eggs

RECIPES

SPRING WELCOME PUNCH

4 ingredients

YIELD: 18–20 punch cups

Equipment: punch bowl and cups

1 pint blackberry-flavored brandy
1 cup lemon juice
1 quart lemon sherbet
1 28-ounce bottle soda water
1 quart cracked ice

Method:
1. Combine brandy and lemon juice in punch bowl.
2. Add lemon sherbet and soda water.
3. Add 1 quart cracked ice and stir. Serve in punch cups.

NUT-COATED CHICKEN BREASTS

4 ingredients

SERVES: 8

Equipment: Dutch oven or large frying pan; kitchen tongs; 9- x 13-inch baking dish

8 whole chicken breasts
2 eggs
2 cups salted mixed nuts
½ pound butter (approximately)

Method:
1. Split chicken breasts in half. Wash carefully, removing skin, and dry with paper towels.
2. Beat eggs and 2 tablespoons water together in a pie plate.
3. Grind nuts in food grinder or chop fine. Pour into a paper sack.
4. Melt about one-half stick of butter over medium heat in large frying pan. When it starts to sizzle, dip a piece of chicken into the egg mixture, then shake in bag of finely chopped nuts. Place in Dutch oven or frying pan. Continue in same manner with remainder of chicken. Do not crowd. It should take 10–15 minutes on each side to brown. Turn with kitchen tongs. Remove to 9- x 13-inch baking dish.
5. Add more butter as you need it for remainder of chicken pieces. Don't allow butter to burn. Turn heat down when necessary.
6. Cover with foil and store in refrigerator.
7. Forty minutes before serving reheat in 325° oven for 30 minutes. Remove foil and brown another 10 minutes. Serve on bed of Fluffy Baked Rice with Oriental Fruit Sauce.

ORIENTAL FRUIT SAUCE

4 ingredients

SERVES: 8

  2 1-pound cans fruit cocktail
  1 tablespoon soy sauce
  ¼ cup lemon juice
  2 tablespoons cornstarch
    Optional: ½ cup preserved ginger, minced

Method:
1. Combine ingredients. Simmer about 5 minutes until mixture thickens.
2. Pass in bowl, to be used on chicken as desired.

CREAMY TOMATO ASPIC LOUIS

4 ingredients

SERVES: 8

Equipment: 1-quart mold (I use Tupperware Gel 'n' Serve.)

  4 eggs
  2 8-ounce bottles Thousand Island dressing
  2 packages unflavored gelatin (I use Knox.)
  2 cups tomato juice
    Optional: iceberg or romaine lettuce

Method:
1. Hard boil eggs.
2. Pour dressing into top section of double boiler over simmering water.
3. Sprinkle gelatin into ¼ cup water. Stir to soften. Add to hot dressing mixture to dissolve. Stir well.
4. Remove from heat. When slightly cooled, add tomato juice and refrigerate until slightly jelled.
5. Peel and slice eggs over aspic mixture, then push gently until they are submerged in aspic.
6. Refrigerate several hours until well set.
7. Unmold and cut in 8 wedges. Serve on bed of shredded iceberg or romaine lettuce, if desired.

DAFFODIL CAKE

3 ingredients and fresh flowers

SERVES : 12 generously

Equipment: angel cake pan

1 18½-ounce package lemon-flavored cake mix (I use Dun-can Hines Lemon Supreme DeLuxe Cake Mix.)
2 egg whites (as called for in directions on package)
1 6½-ounce package lemon-flavored frosting mix (I use Betty Crocker Sunkist Lemon Fluff Frosting Mix.)
3 or 4 fresh daffodils and green leaves

Method:
1. Make cake in angel food pan as directed on package. Cool.
2. Make frosting as directed on package. Frost cake when it is thoroughly cool.
3. Insert small jar in center hole of cake. (A baby food jar works perfectly.) Carefully fill with water. Arrange 3 or 4 daffodils and green leaves in jar.

Note: This cake makes a pretty Easter table centerpiece when placed on a footed lazy susan to give it height. Green leaves and/or fresh flowers around the outside gives a pretty effect.

HOMEMADE CHOCOLATE EASTER EGGS

4 ingredients

YIELD: 12

*Equipment: plastic egg carton and double boiler**

  1 4-ounce jar maraschino cherries
  ½ pound butter
  2 pounds confectioner's sugar
  2 7½-ounce packages semi-sweet chocolate chips and
     chopped walnuts. (I use Baker's Chips 'n Nuts.)

  *If you don't happen to have a double boiler, use a regular saucepan set in a large frying pan of simmering water.

Method:
1. Spoon 2 tablespoons maraschino cherry juice into large bowl. Add finely cut-up cherries.
2. Melt butter and mix with cherries and juice. Add chopped nuts if desired.
3. Combine confectioner's sugar with butter mixture and work together with your hands as if making pie dough. It needs to be the consistency of butter cream candy.
4. Shape into eggs, using ½ cup each time, by rolling mixture between buttered hands, shaping one end a little smaller than the other.
5. Set them on end in egg carton. To harden, set in refrigerator several hours.
6. Melt chocolate morsels in top part of double boiler, over simmering water.
7. Dip one end of each candy egg into melted chocolate, then set back in egg carton. When all have been dipped, return carton to refrigerator for an hour or two.
8. When thoroughly hardened, dip the other end into melted chocolate. (A pair of kitchen tongs works well here.) Return to refrigerator.

Note: If you are a cake-decorating buff, you can let your imagination run wild. Flowers, leaves, birds, scallops, swirls all add to their appeal. However, the candy is just as delicious undecorated.

TIPS FOR PREPARING AND SERVING Place punch bowl on coffee table in living room. Encircle the base with short green sprigs, such as ivy or any green plant or fern which lasts well out of water. Insert small, fresh flowers every 2 or 3 inches in among the greens. Place punch cups, punch ladle, and cocktail napkins nearby.

A dining-room hutch cabinet is very convenient for a serve-yourself buffet. For this particular menu, I place a stack of heated plates at the left side of shelf. Next to plates, I place the rice casserole, then the chicken, then the fruit sauce. Guests serve themselves, then find places at the fully set table.

The aspic salad is placed just above the forks at each guest's place. I find crescent-shaped glass salad plates practical. They are great space-savers as they curve around the dinner plate.

Rolls are passed at table.

The Daffodil Cake doubles as centerpiece.

The Chocolate Easter Eggs are made several days in advance. When time permits, I decorate them, using a can of cake decorating frosting. To add a personal touch, write each guest's name or initials with one of the cake decorator tips, then set eggs in small baskets on table to act as place markers.

SETTING THE SCENE

SUGGESTIONS FOR EASTER CENTERPIECES

A bright-colored Easter basket, very inexpensive at this time of year, filled with lovely spring flowers—tulips, hyacinths, narcissuses, irises, and possibly a flowering branch or two. If children are present, a saucy rabbit leaning against the basket will intrigue them; or you could place baby chicks, tiny bunnies, or little ducks here and there among the flowers or wired to the basket handle.

Girls especially will be entranced with an Easter bonnet tree. Bare branches are stuck into floral clay which has been fastened securely to the bottom of a flower bowl or Easter basket. The hats are from the doll-clothes department of the ten-cent store. Remove the trimming and replace it with velvet ribbons and tiny flowers or other trim of good quality. You'll find glue more satisfactory and speedier than trying to sew on the trimming. Hang these little beauties on the branches.

A bright-colored sun hat with a brim, often available for about $1, makes a fetching centerpiece when used this way: Cut small holes in crown of hat. Fill a small mixing bowl with florist's foam (available from florists or florists' supply houses).

Place the bowl underneath the hat. Poke flowers through the holes into the foam. The flowers should just rest lightly on the crown of hat to resemble trimming. If you wish, add a satin band and bow.

Nothing is prettier than a platter or basket heaped with gaily decorated Easter eggs. If you take the time and effort to blow them out and wash them carefully before decorating, they can be used for many years. Blown-out eggs are light enough to be suspended from branches or a piece of driftwood.

TO BLOW OUT EGGS

Let eggs come to room temperature. Set egg in an egg cup, or empty egg carton, end up. With an ice pick or other pointed utensil, peck gently at the top until the shell is broken. With tweezers, pick off broken fragments of shell. The hole should be about $\frac{1}{4}$ inch in diameter. Turn the other end up and do the same thing.

Standing over the sink, blow gently into one of the small holes. The egg will then come out the opposite end. When it is empty, run water into it, shake gently, and let the water run out until clear. Decorate as you wish. You'll find the shell surprisingly sturdy if you're cautious. Insert a small ornament hanger (the type used to hang Christmas-tree balls) in each of the holes if you wish to hang them or suspend something from them.

ENTERTAINMENT

BUNNY HUNT FOR TOTS Here's an adaptation of that old children's game, Blind Man's Buff.

One child is "It," and in this case, let's call him Bugs Bunny. Bugs is blindfolded, then slowly counts out loud, "1-2-3-4-5." During this time he must whirl around two or three times while the children run here and there around him. They must not leave the room or playing area.

After the count of 5, he calls, "Bunnies stop, wherever you are." At this command, players freeze. They mustn't move another step. With hands held out in front, Bugs moves cautiously on a hunt for a bunny. Although players may not move their feet, they are allowed to duck or bend sideways to try to keep out of Bugs' reach. When Bugs touches or runs into a player, he yells, "Gotcha!" The blindfold is then tied on the new Bugs Bunny.

You'll find that children will want to play this again and again. The weird positions in which contestants freeze, plus the element of suspense of watching Bugs stalking his prey, bring on shivers and giggles and will keep children amused for quite a while.

ICEBREAKER TREASURE HUNT As soon as all guests arrive, give each one an entry sheet similar to this:

Instructions: 1. Find the person described and write name opposite the description.

2. When all names are entered take this sheet to hostess. First one with complete correct list wins prize.

(1) A man with shoe lace untied
(2) A lady with one earring
(3) A man with an odd sock
(4) Tallest man present
(5) A lady with wrist watch on right arm
(6) A man with only one sock
(7) Shortest lady present
(8) A man with ring on thumb
(9) A lady wearing two shades of nail polish
(10) A man wearing red suspenders
(11) A lady wearing a lace garter
(12) Man with the bluest eyes

Of course, you may make up any list you like. Put a close friend in charge of the game so that she can take each person aside as he arrives and attach the article or tell him about the game so that they are in cahoots. All guests participate as each one knows only about his own part in it.

THE EASTER BASKET SURPRISE Here's a game that's fun to play, doesn't take too long, and gets the party off to a merry start.

You will need:

1. 6 or 7 gaily wrapped prizes, preferably gag-type. (Wrap them.)
2. Basket or other container in which to put prizes.
3. One pair dice, preferably the jumbo size which measures about two inches across.

This game is best played sitting in a circle on the floor. Each player takes his turn throwing the dice. The object is to get two of a kind—two fours, two sixes, etc. When a player succeeds in doing this, he gets his choice of the prizes in the basket, but is not to open it. When all the prizes are gone, the game speeds up considerably. A timer or alarm clock is set to go off in five minutes. The game proceeds as before except that those who roll two of a kind are permitted to take a prize from any other player. The faster the game, the more opportunity to win somebody's prize from him. When the alarm rings, the game is over and players open and keep the prize or prizes in their possession. I've seen even very sophisticated people play this game as if their very lives depended on it. There'll be shrieks of "Hurry up, hurry up, before the time runs out!" You'll see. It really is fun, and a grand ice-breaker.

Ideas for prizes: Self-winding spaghetti fork, pair of false eyelashes, freak wig, life-size pin-ups, funny hats or caps, huge diamond stickpin, mink tie, unusual beer can opener, etc. All items may be found in joke stores.

Mother's Day
Breakfast in the Garden

FOR 6

8:30 to 9:30 A.M.

In many families it has become a tradition for the children to plan and prepare at least one meal in Mother's honor on her day.

Following is an ideal breakfast for the children to host. It is very easy to prepare and everything is ready at the same time. I often use this one myself when I have house guests.

MENU

*Mixed Fruit Compote topped with Mint Sherbet
Muffin Tin 15-Minute Breakfast
*Baked Eggs in Cream
Brown 'n Serve Sausage Patties
*Glazed Pineapple Rings
Hot Biscuits and Honey
Coffee   Milk

RECIPES

MIXED FRUIT COMPOTE

2 ingredients

SERVES: 6

2 packages quick-thaw fruit (I use Birdseye.)
1 pint mint sherbet
   Optional: Sprigs of fresh mint

Method:
1. Thaw fruit.
2. Scoop approximately ⅓ cup sherbet over each serving.
3. Tuck sprig of fresh mint into each, if desired. Serve at once.

BAKED EGGS IN CREAM

4 ingredients

SERVES : 6

Equipment: 2 twelve-cup muffin tins. One muffin tin is used for sausages, the other for both eggs and pineapple slices

2 tablespoons butter (¼ stick)
6 eggs
⅓ cup Half-and-Half
1 teaspoon seasoned salt, approximately (I use Lawry's Seasoned Salt.)

Method:
1. Place 1 teaspoon butter in each of 6 cups of one muffin tin. Place in oven a few moments to melt.
2. Break 1 egg into each cup.
3. Spoon 1 tablespoon Half-and-Half over each egg.
4. Sprinkle lightly with seasoned salt.

GLAZED PINEAPPLE RINGS

3 ingredients

SERVES : 6

2 tablespoons butter
2 tablespoons brown sugar
1 16-ounce can pineapple slices (Apricot halves may be used in place of pineapple.)

Method:
1. Allow butter to soften slightly in a bowl.
2. Add brown sugar and stir together. Spoon mixture into the remaining six empty muffin cups.
3. Lay a pineapple slice on top of brown sugar and butter mixture.
4. Bake 12–15 minutes at 375°. Eggs determine the length of time. They should be slightly soft in the center because they continue cooking in the hot pan.

Brown'n Serve patties are placed in the second muffin tin and baked at same time as eggs and pineapple.

TIPS FOR PREPARING AND SERVING　　Defrost Mixed Fruit Compote according to directions on package. Keep chilled in refrigerator. At serving time add a scoop of mint sherbet to each serving, place on a tray, and carry to table which is already set in garden.

Place Muffin Tin 15-Minute Breakfast in oven just before you call others to breakfast. Set timer for 12 minutes so that you can keep a close watch on the eggs. They should be slightly soft in the center when you remove from oven. Set muffin tins on a tray. Take to garden to serve.

Bake Hot Biscuits at same temperature and for same length of time as the other items. This gives them a nice crusty texture and eliminates a too-doughy center which sometimes occurs at higher temperatures.

SETTING THE SCENE

Daisy place mats are very effective, particularly on a dark tablecloth. They can be made from construction paper or shelf liner. Make a 12-petal daisy pattern out of light cardboard about 9 inches in diameter. Place on white construction paper. Trace around the pattern, then cut. Use black gummed paper for the centers.

The children will enjoy making a flower lei for Mother. A pile of small gifts in the center of the table with the lei encircling them makes a pretty centerpiece.

All that is needed is a quantity of flowers which last well out of water, such as pompon chrysanthemums, bachelor buttons, pinks, carnations, marguerites, asters, ivy geranium blossoms. Remove the stems. A double thread about 2 yards long, preferably of nylon or embroidery cotton, is also needed, and a strong needle such as a darning needle about 2 inches long.

Push the needle through the heart of a flower. Take care that they are all facing one way. When several are strung, push them to the end of the thread, starting a row of continuous blossoms. Continue until entire thread is filled.

Tie the ends together, and there is a beautiful ''necklace'' of flowers. When breakfast is over, the children slip the lei over Mother's head, then give her a tender kiss, first on one cheek, then the other, as Hawaiians do.

A Morning Coffee
Anticipates the Stork

<small>FOR</small> 12

10:00 to 11:30 A.M.

Three cheers for the person who dreamed up the idea of the morning coffee party. There are many reasons for its popularity.

It is the easiest possible party for occasions such as entertaining a relative or out-of-town guest, showering a friend, introducing a new neighbor, hosting a committee meeting, introducing a new bride, or honoring a birthday.

Your menu need not be extensive—3 or 4 items and plenty of coffee.

It is a short party—say 10 to 11:30. Mothers of school-age children are freer at that time.

Regarding invitations, you may telephone them or send them through the mail. For written invitations, I often use fold-over note paper. There are ever so many beautiful designs from which to choose and then you are free to word it the way you wish. Here is an example:

Stork Shower

in honor of Mary Taylor
Friday morning, May 1st
at 10 o'clock

Please reply   *10 Park Avenue*
Rosalind Mansfield   *Parkdale*
433–1234

---

10 to 10:30 A.M.: Coffee and light refreshments
10:30 to 11 A.M.: Games
11 to 11:30 A.M.: Gifts are opened

MENU

Frosty Fruit Juice Cooler
*Cheese Snacks
*Banana Quickbread with Chiquita Banana Filling
*Chocolate Mint Meringues
*Nut and Coconut Macaroons
Coffee   Iced Tea

RECIPES

CHEESE SNACKS

4 ingredients

YIELD: 24

Equipment: cookie sheet or cake pans

½ cup butter (1 stick)
½ teaspoon paprika, or 3 to 4 drops Tabasco sauce
2 cups sharp cheddar cheese
1 cup flour

Method:
1. Allow butter to come to room temperature. Add paprika or Tabasco sauce.
2. Grate cheese. Blend in seasoned butter.
3. Add flour and stir.
4. Work together with hands as though you were making pie dough.
5. Pinch off a small amount, about a rounded teaspoonful, and roll into a ball. Flatten with heel of hand and arrange on ungreased cookie sheet.
6. Bake in 325° oven for 20 minutes or until lightly browned.

BANANA QUICKBREAD
WITH CHIQUITA BANANA FILLING

2 ingredients

YIELD : 1 5- x 9-inch loaf

1 package banana quickbread mix (I use Pillsbury.)
1 package Chiquita Banana Frosting

Method:
1. Bake quickbread according to directions on package. Cool thoroughly.
2. Cut in thin slices.
3. Make frosting according to directions on package.
4. Spread a slice of quickbread with frosting. Cover with a second slice.
5. Cut in 2 or 3 pieces.

CHOCOLATE MINT MERINGUES

4 ingredients

YIELD : 4 dozen

Equipment: cookie sheet

  3 egg whites
  1 cup confectioner's sugar
  ⅓ cup saltine cracker crumbs (approximately 8 saltines)
  1 6-ounce package semi-sweet chocolate mint morsels

Method:
1. Heat oven to 350°.
2. Beat egg whites until stiff.
3. Add sugar slowly, 1 tablespoon at a time, beating constantly.
4. Fold in cracker crumbs and melted chocolate.
5. Drop by rounded teaspoonfuls 1½ inches apart on greased cookie sheet.
6. Bake 13–15 minutes, until firm to touch.

NUT AND COCONUT MACAROONS

4 ingredients

YIELD : 4½ dozen

Equipment: cookie sheet

  2 8-ounce packages moist, shredded coconut
  1 15-ounce can sweetened, condensed milk (I use Borden's Eagle brand.)
  ½ cup nuts, finely chopped
  2 teaspoons vanilla

A Morning Coffee Anticipates the Stork ❧ *67*

Method:

1. Heat oven to 350°.
2. Combine ingredients and mix well.
3. Drop from teaspoon, 1 inch apart, onto well-greased cookie sheet.
4. Bake 10 minutes or until delicately browned. Remove from sheet at once.

TIPS FOR PREPARING AND SERVING   Early in the day set table, with tray, spoons, and cups at one end and tray, iced tea glasses, iced tea spoons at other. At each side of table have available a stack of salad plates and luncheon-size napkins.

Make Fruit Juice Cooler and store in quart jars in refrigerator. When guests arrive, pour Cooler into 6-ounce glasses and set on tray with cocktail napkins. Offer as soon as guests are seated.

Arrange each of the following on separate serving dish or platter—the Cheese Snacks, Banana Quickbread with Chiquita Banana Filling, Chocolate Mint Meringues, Nut and Coconut Macaroons. Wrap each serving dish in Saran Wrap or slip into a Baggie to keep fresh.

SETTING THE SCENE

Not knowing whether the baby will be in the ''sugar and spice'' or the ''snips and snails'' category, it's advisable to bypass pink or blue as a color scheme. Sunshine yellow is pretty. You might consider making a tablecloth of white dimity with sprigs of yellow roses.

Baby-doll clothes (available in toy departments) hanging on a clothesline make an amusing centerpiece. You will need 2 dowels about 12 inches high, set in small blocks of wood or styrofoam circles. Miniature clothespins and line are available in most department store notions departments. The set is designed for travelers, but works very well for this purpose.

Any of the following would be a suitable container for the gifts: bassinet, antique cradle, decorated baby buggy, or beribboned clothes basket.

For bulky gifts, fold a large bed sheet like a 3-cornered diaper, place the gifts inside, and secure it with a tremendous safety pin, then drag the bundle unceremoniously into the room and lay it at the feet of the prospective mother.

A close friend should assist in disposing of wrappings and making sure that the card is enclosed with each gift before it is passed from guest to guest to examine.

ENTERTAINMENT

Don't worry too much about entertainment for a group of this sort because they're as sociable as a basket of kittens! However, games and contests will make a better party. Here are several which are fun.

BABY CONTEST   This promises to be one of the high spots, if you are able to assemble the "props." The game committee collects a baby picture from each guest and mounts them all on a large piece of paper with a number over each.

Keep the display covered until ready to use. Pencils and papers are distributed, the contest is explained, the exhibit unveiled.

Guests try to identify the baby pictures, marking them down on their individual sheets, then the sheets are turned in. The player who guesses the greatest number wins.

TELEGRAM GAME   Each contestant draws a letter from a hat. She then must compose a 10-word telegram announcing the baby's birth, each word beginning with the letter she has drawn. If her letter is "C," it might be as follows:

> Cute cheerful cuddly cherub called Connie cooing constantly captivates Coopers.

FORTUNES   Here are a few jingles appropriate for a baby shower. One could be attached to each gift. As the honored guest opens each package, she reads the donor's fortune.

Examples:

> *A happy girl you'll always be,*
> *You won the heart that loves but thee.*
> *Children galore, around you buzzin'*
> *Oh well, they're cheaper by the dozen!*

> *For you I see a household piled*
> *With fourteen children, loud and wild,*
> *Two birds, a cat, a wire-haired terrier,*
> *But remember, dear, the more the merrier.*

It's fun and easy to compose simple jingles. Try it and see.

STORK BINGO   Here's an amusing Bingo game.

On 16 small pieces of paper, write the following 16 words: Baby, Bootees, Lullaby, Clothesline, Carriage, Bassinet, Bottle, Triplets, Rattle, Stork, Talcum, Mamma, Daddy, Toys, Baby Sitter, Formula. Place slips in a bag or bowl.

Hand out a pencil and piece of paper approximately 8 inches square to each player. Ask her to draw 3 lines across and 3 lines down at equal distances. This will give 16 squares. (Hostess can prepare the score sheets ahead of time if she wishes.)

Hostess draws a slip from the bowl and calls out the word. Guests write the word in any one of the squares. She draws a second slip and calls it out. Guests write that word in another square. As she calls out the words, she drops the squares in a second bowl.

After all the squares have been filled, she mixes them up well, and starts drawing them a second time. This time the guests make a cross over the word. The first player to get 4 crosses vertically, horizontally, or diagonally calls out "Bingo!" and gets a prize.

Summer
Parties

🌽 *JUNE*

🍲 *JULY*

🌽 *AUGUST*

Anniversary Open House

FOR 50

6:00 to 8:30 P.M.

During the busy years of raising a family, we are prone to forget the importance of ''The Day,'' as anniversaries roll around so quickly. Suddenly we stop in amazement. Can it possibly be 25 years? or 35? or 40?

Wedding anniversaries can be gala affairs and deserve to be celebrated. These occasions give great pleasure to the bridal couple and to family and friends, especially the ones who attended the wedding so many years ago.

If sons and daughters or other relatives or friends give the party, it is perfectly proper to send engraved invitations. These are readily available at stationers, department stores, and many gift shops. For this event guests usually send gifts, traditionally silver for the twenty-fifth anniversary and gold for the fiftieth.

An open house on a Sunday afternoon, say from 3:00 to 5:00, is a pleasant way to gather old friends together. Open house invitations are readily available. No mention of the anniversary is made.

There are many couples who prefer celebrating the event in their own home. This was the case recently on the occasion of my husband's and my silver anniversary. We preferred not to send formal invitations and sent instead colorful invitations which merely said:

> Cocktails   6:00 P.M.
> Buffet Supper   7:30 P.M.

followed by pertinent information as to date, address, telephone number, etc.

Invite as many guests as possible who attended the wedding, particularly members of the original wedding party. If possible, include the clergyman who performed the ceremony.

Try to send invitations at least 2 weeks in advance.

Here's an important suggestion: Even if it's necessary for you to make all the arrangements and do the cooking, you should be free to welcome and chat with your guests. Try to get someone else to supervise in the kitchen.

MENU

Wedding Anniversary Punch
*Rainbow Ribbon Sandwiches
*Miniature Open-Faced Broiled Hamburgers
*Nutty Brown Bread Half Moons
Salted Nuts   White Mints
Wedding Cake
Coffee   Tea

RECIPES

RAINBOW RIBBON SANDWICHES

4 ingredients

YIELD: approximately 96

   3 loaves pastel-colored bread* (I use pale pink, pale green, and pale yellow.)
   6 7½-ounce cans crabmeat
1½–2 cups salad dressing (I use Kraft Miracle Whip.)
   3 6-ounce packages cream cheese with chives

*You can ''special order'' colored bread from the majority of bakeries on advance notice. Very pale colors are prettiest.

Method:

Early in the day:

1. Remove crusts from 4 sides and ends of bread.
2. Slice bread horizontally (*not* vertically, as is usually done) in ½-inch slices. You will usually get about 6 slices, measuring approximately 4 inches x 12 inches x ½ inch. (Obliging bakers will usually remove crusts and cut bread for you—so easy with their equipment.)
3. Remove any cartilage from crabmeat. Drain well, then squeeze out any additional moisture with paper towels.
4. Combine crabmeat with salad dressing. Set aside.
5. Let cream cheese come to room temperature. Mash with fork until of spreading consistency. You may have to add a tablespoon or two of water.
6. To assemble:
   Place a layer of green bread on bread board and spread it with ⅙ of the cream cheese.
   Place a layer of yellow bread on top of cream cheese and spread with ⅙ of the crab mixture.
   Top with a layer of pink bread.
   Wrap tightly in Saran Wrap and store in refrigerator for several hours.
   Repeat with remainder of ingredients.

You will have 6 loaves of bread. An hour or two before party, cut in ¾-inch slices. An electric knife comes in handy here. You should get about 16 sandwiches from each loaf.

Arrange on platter or serving plate and cover plate and sandwiches with Saran Wrap and return to refrigerator.

Note: Despite the length of instuctions, this is a simple task and I doubt if it will take an hour of your time. Imagine how much more difficult to make 96 individual sandwiches! These are delicious and beautiful to behold.

MINIATURE OPEN-FACED BROILED HAMBURGERS

4 ingredients

YIELD: 100

Equipment: cookie sheets

25 slices white bread
2 eggs
3 pounds extra-lean ground round steak, ground to order if possible
1 cup ketchup (I use Heinz.)

Method:
1. Cut 4 small rounds out of each piece of bread with small biscuit cutter. Place in single layer on cookie sheets.
2. Beat eggs until fluffy. Combine with ground beef in large bowl. Scoop out 1 rounded teaspoon and roll between palms to make small meat balls, then flatten slightly. Sprinkle with salt and pepper.
3. Place a patty on each bread round.
4. Top each with approximately $\frac{1}{4}$ teaspoon ketchup.
5. Broil in preheated oven for 4–5 minutes or until slightly brown.
6. Arrange on serving plate and serve at once, piping hot.

NUTTY BROWN BREAD HALF MOONS

4 ingredients

YIELD: 40 half moons

2 1-pound cans brown bread (I use B & M.)
1 8-ounce package cream cheese (I use Philadelphia.)
4 tablespoons frozen orange juice, undiluted
2 cups walnuts, finely chopped

Method:
1. Remove both ends of cans of brown bread. Using one of the can ends, push out loaf. Refrigerate until well chilled.
2. Let cream cheese come to room temperature.
3. Add undiluted orange juice.
4. Cream with fork until of spreadable consistency. Add chopped nuts and mix well.
5. Cut brown bread in thin slices, approximately ¼ inch thick.
6. Spread cream cheese mixture on one-half of the slices.
7. Top with remaining slices and wrap "sandwiches" in Saran Wrap.
8. At serving time, cut each in half to resemble a half moon. Arrange on serving plate.

WEDDING CAKES

If you are planning a large party, it will probably be wise to order your cake from a caterer. A 3-tiered wedding cake is a thing of beauty and practical as well. It serves two purposes: acts as centerpiece on your cake table and provides the main item on your menu.

HOME-BAKED WEDDING CAKES

Here are suggestions for cakes which may be made at home. Appropriately decorated and displayed, they can be just as festive and delicious as lavish cakes made professionally.

You can make Heart-Shaped Layer Cakes with white icing, trimmed with silver dragées, and a small white candle for each year.

Another possibility is a Confetti Cake: large round layers with confetti-like trim circling the top of cake. Use fluffy 7-minute frosting. For the trim, cut green and red maraschino cherries into very tiny pieces, and arrange in a 2-inch circle on outer rim of top of cake.

Other suitable emblems for decorating the top: silver or gold slipper, wedding bells, hearts, roses, orange blossoms, the numbers "25" or "50" or whatever the anniversary.

Either rose water or orange-flower water makes a delicious flavoring for wedding cakes.

Wrapped in foil and baked into the cake, tiny favors add a festive fun touch to the celebration. Finding a coin means wealth; a tiny wishbone, good luck; a ring, the next one married. If cost is no object, these tiny favors may be of gold or silver. They can usually be found at jewelry counters among the charms that go on charm bracelets. However, the ten-cent variety will be welcomed just as enthusiastically by the finders. (These favors can be inserted in the bottom of the cake after it is baked, if you prefer.)

TIPS FOR PREPARING AND SERVING   Place punch at one end of dining table on a large tray, with punch cups and cocktail napkins nearby. Usually a relative or close friend pours. If possible, use a long-handled punch ladle. A second punch bowl could be placed in the living room, possibly on a large coffee table. A member of the family or close friend could be appointed to keep punch bowls replenished.

Arrange sandwiches, hamburgers, and nut bread on china or silver platters and set on dining table.

Place wedding cake on separate cake table.

Place coffee and tea on one tray at opposite end of table. Nearby, place cups, saucers, spoons, cream, sugar, lemon slices, and luncheon-size napkins.

SETTING THE SCENE

Decorate your home as for a wedding with fresh flowers and lighted candles. During cold weather, a wood fire glowing in your fireplace adds a cheerful note, with the mantel massed with greens and flickering white candles.

Silvered ivy leaves, silvered fruit, or clusters of purple grapes arranged in a wreath are attractive on a dark table. Place a candle in a low silver candlestick in the center.

Fill heart-shaped cake pans with silver leaves and small white flowers. Leaves extend over the edge to disguise the pan.

I've always thought the mistletoe custom much too fascinating to confine to the Yuletide season alone. What more appropriate time to have a Kissing Ring than at an anniversary celebration? Let's add as much gaiety to this party as possible.

Kissing Ring: Cover two embroidery hoops with silver or gold foil. Place one inside the other at right angles to form a sphere. Wire together and suspend gold or silver bell inside. Attach gold or silver satin bows and suspend from doorway or light fixture. Explain its purpose; your guests will take over from there.

For a wedding cake table at a spring reception we attended, a round, pale pink, sprigged organdy cloth, floor length, was used on a small round table. It had been placed over a darker pink "petticoat."

A 3-tiered white wedding cake with roses of palest pink graced the center of the table. A pair of 5-branched candelabra flanked the cake.

A colorful arrangement of spring flowers—yellow miniature irises and pink roses—was in a glass epergne which fit into the center candleholder, giving the entire table height and importance. Very pale pink candles were used. Encircling the bases of cake and candelabra were sprigs of ivy and tiny pink flowers.

A silver cake knife, a stack of small white and silver paper plates, luncheon-size paper napkins of good quality, and forks were placed on each side of cake.

The table was placed against one wall to allow more room for guests to circulate.

Paper accessories of good quality are used at most large receptions. Department stores, stationers, and gift shops carry a good selection of paper napkins in various sizes, either plain or monogrammed.

Nicely designed clear plastic punch cups and small plates are available at low cost, or china and glassware can be rented from a party rental company if you prefer.

ENTERTAINMENT

Music adds so much gaiety to any party, and is particularly enjoyable at an occasion like this.

If budget permits, consider engaging one or two professional musicians. At a recent golden anniversary, a violinist and accordionist played and strolled among the guests, featuring music which was popular fifty years ago, and also songs which have been particular favorites of the bridal couple throughout the years. If professional entertainment is out of the question, purchase a long-playing record or two. Some of the most beautiful music ever written was composed in the twenties.

Perhaps you have a guitarist, pianist, or accordionist in your group. Request songs which were hits at the time of your marriage.

Some of the songs popular in the forties are ''One Dozen Roses,'' ''Tangerine,'' ''That Old Black Magic,'' ''The White Cliffs of Dover,'' ''White Christmas,'' ''You'd Be So Nice to Come Home to,'' ''People Will Say We're in Love,'' and ''Speak Low.'' Most important of all, ask them to feature *your* song.

A guest register makes a lovely memento. Buy a handsome bridal book which has spaces for pictures of reception guests as well as of the bridal couple. Color Polaroid pictures can be taken of the guests and immediately entered in the album, then guests can inscribe greetings beside the picture. This is one of the most precious mementos a couple can receive. One picture can be of the couple gazing at their original wedding picture. Other favorite shots are the bridal couple welcoming guests, the cutting of the cake, and the toast to the ''bride and bridegroom.'' (If the best man is present, he will make the toast. otherwise any close friend may do it.)

If you have your original bride's book, place it on display. If there is enough space left, have your anniversary guests sign it. A young relative might be given this responsibility.

Display your wedding gown if it is still in good condition. By all means wear it if it still fits you.

If gifts are put on display. cards of donors should be removed just as you do at a wedding.

Indian Birthday Supper

5 :00 to 8 :00 P.M.

There are probably more children's birthday parties given than all other types of entertaining combined. Even busy mothers, who do little entertaining otherwise, manage to do "something special" for Johnny's birthday.

To a child, his birthday is a very important and exciting date. Not only is he one whole year older, he is the "King of the Castle" for that one special day.

Boys and girls have always been fascinated by tales of the American Indian, so we've decided to describe a birthday party with an Indian theme which we feel will be exciting to both guests and "birthday child." Be sure to allow him to help prepare for the party. Maybe he could get a friend to help make invitations and decorations. The anticipation and preparation are often as much fun as the party itself.

Clever wigwam invitations with Indian designs on the front can be made in a short while at little expense. From construction paper or plain white stationery, cut round pieces measuring 9 inches in diameter. Fold in half, then cut in two. Each half circle makes one invitation. Fold in semi-circles. In center of front section make a little upside-down V to represent entrance. Decorate front with Indian motifs such as arrows, fish, birds, crescent moons, etc.

Write invitation inside.

Indian Birthday Supper 🎯 81

KI YI KI YI KI YI

HEAP BIG POWWOW

Here's the message—I'll be brief—
Every tribe send mighty chief,
Shoshone, Ute, Blackfoot, Apache,
Kiowa, Sioux, Cheyenne, Cherokee.
Smoke signals gave me this word—
We meet at sign of Thunderbird.

If you want to make it a costume affair, ask each guest to wear lots of beads and a blanket. (In this way they'll have something to sit on during the games.)

ℳENU

Kickapoo Joy Juice (Cold spicy tomato juice cocktail.
I use Campbell's V-8 Juice.)
*Chili Dogs
Maize (corn on the cob)
Wild Roots (carrot and celery sticks and scallions)
*Indian War Dance Birthday Cake   Hot Chocolate

ℛECIPES

CHILI DOGS

4 ingredients

SERVES : 10

1-pound can chili con carne
10 frankfurters
10 frankfurter buns
¼ cup onion, minced

Method:
1. Heat chili and franks.
2. Toast buns.
3. Place franks in buns and spoon on chili. Sprinkle with minced onion.

INDIAN WAR DANCE
BIRTHDAY CAKE

2 ingredients

SERVES: 10–12 generously

Equipment: layer cake pans; 10–12 plastic Indian figures*

1 18½-ounce package cake mix (birthday child's favorite)
1 16½-ounce can ready-to-spread frosting

   *Plastic Indian figures are readily available in most ten-cent stores and toy departments at a nominal price.

Method:
1. Make cake according to directions. Cool completely.
2. Frost bottom layer. Place other layer upside down on first layer so that tops are together. Frost top layer.
3. Wash Indian figures carefully in hot, soapy water. Dry thoroughly. Place 10 or 12 of them, standing up, around the outer edge of cake, all facing the same way as if they were doing a war dance.

Note: An alternate idea is to lay 2 Indian feather headbands flat on a table and place the cake between them. It will give a sunburst effect—very pretty with all the bright-colored feathers.

TIPS FOR PREPARING AND SERVING   Cover 2 card tables with plastic cloths. Place the tables flat, in center of teepee, without unfolding legs. Braves and squaws sit around edge of tables. Food is placed on tables and passed.

Serve birthday cake at dusk just before the end of party. Kickapoo Joy Juice, apples, nuts in the shell, or popcorn could be available for the weary warriors during the games.

SETTING THE SCENE

The backyard would be the perfect location and would keep the confusion and clutter outside.

Center of operations should be a tent or teepee. Ideally, there should be 2 or 3. Possibly you could borrow a couple of extras from friends. Several tents set up next to each other give a fine effect; the children could make up some Indian designs to tape to the tents. Indian symbols, in bright colors, would also be effective taped or tacked to fences. Stick-on paper in vivid colors is now readily available.

Prior to the party, make up some large name tags on which are written Indian names. Place the girls' names in one bag, the boys' names in another. All the girls are princesses and all the boys chiefs. Possibly the birthday host could be Chief Rain-in-the-Face. Other names are Chief Running Bear, Chief Hiawatha, Crazy Horse, Red Cloud, Black Hawk, Thunder Cloud, Bald Eagle, Fire Maker. For girls, names could be Princess Willow Wand, Princess Laughing Brook, Blue Sky, Prairie Flower, West Wind, Pocahontas.

During the party, everyone must be called by his or her Indian name, which should be pinned or stuck on in plain view.

ENTERTAINMENT

INDIAN HEADBAND GAME   Preliminary preparations can be done by the birthday child ahead of time.

Cut a headband for each person out of material cut on the bias. This will make them fit securely. Cut 20 slits in each. Slits should be about one inch apart and about one inch long.

Cut 10 feathers out of construction paper, each in a different bright color, for each band. Feathers should be about 7 inches long and ¾ inch wide at the base. (Several feathers may be cut at one time.) On the red feathers mark 1, 2, 3, 4, 5, 6, etc. Do the same with the other colors. Place each color in a separate bag, then shake them up. Make a duplicate set of slips and place in bowl.

Players sit in a circle, legs crossed Indian fashion. Each is given a headband and told to draw one feather from each bag so that he will have 10 feathers in all, each a different color. Chief Rain-in-the-Face draws a slip from the bowl.

He calls out, ''Who has red feather number 3? Insert it in your band.'' Then he draws again and says, ''Who has green feather number 7?'' And so it goes until all the feathers are in the bands. (If you wish, you may give a small prize to the Indian who completes his headband first.) The play goes on until all slits are filled with feathers. Each now puts on his headband. Ends may be tied or stapled together for a good fit.

WILD GAME HUNT   Buy 2 packages of gummed seals; there are 48 in a package. (There is one called Forest Animals.) Thumbtack them to fences, garden implements, window boxes, etc., in the backyard. Players go on a hunt for the stickers. Allow 5–10 minutes. (Give each player a bag for seals and tacks.)

They score like this: for each bear found, count 6 points; for every deer, count 5; fox, 4; raccoon, 3; beaver, 2; rabbit, 1. Award a fresh package of seals to the winner.

Note: These gummed seals also may be used on place cards, as decorations for packages, and for sealing envelopes, such as the envelope used to enclose party invitation.

REDSKIN WALKING RACE—Line all contestants up—a squaw, then a brave, etc. In this race one foot is placed directly in front of the other, with heel touching toe on other foot each time. Race should be about 25 feet long. A bag of yellow and black candy corn is awarded to the winner.

STAGECOACH   Several days ahead, Chief Rain-in-the-Face and 2 or 3 of his pals make up a horror story using the following words: Indian Princess, Hiawatha, Indian tribe, braves, squaws, wicked Indian scout, Land of the Sky Blue Water, old Indian chieftain, wigwam, tom-tom, smoke signals, war dance, jealous maiden, handsome brave, bows and arrows, tomahawk, massacre, papoose, peace pipe, moccasins, war paint, feathered headdresses, Indian village.

At game time, each guest is assigned a word from the list above. The narrator starts reading the story.

Let's say that a player is given the word "wigwam." Each time that word is read he jumps up, runs around his blanket, then sits down again. Whenever the word "Indian" is used, everyone jumps up and runs around his blanket.

In the confusion, the narrator tries to grab someone's blanket. If successful, that person has to act as narrator until he's able to grab a blanket. Your story might go something like this:

> Once upon a time there lived a beautiful Indian Princess. She lived in a wigwam in the Land of the Sky Blue Water. The beautiful Indian Princess was in love with the handsome brave, Hiawatha. This made her wicked Indian father wild with rage, as the handsome brave Hiawatha was a member of an enemy tribe. He sent up smoke signals ordering a council of war and hundreds of braves assembled for the powwow in the Land of the Sky Blue Water.

Space doesn't permit an entire story, but I'm sure that you can go on from there. Limit it to about 500 words.

An alternate idea is to find an exciting Indian story at the library. Children take turns reading from the book.

Children's Midsummer African Safari Supper

5 :00 to 7 :30 P.M.

An African Safari is getting under way,
We're going on a jungle hunt
This coming Saturday.
Come dressed as big game hunter
In helmet, shorts, and beard;
Or come as painted savage
In feathered costume weird.

Boys and girls from 8 to 12 love adventure and surely will get a thrill out of receiving an invitation like this. By all means let your young man or lady help with the preparations. Two or three young people working together will get as much fun out of planning and decorating as out of the party itself. You'll be surprised, too, with the number of good ideas that they come up with.

To escape the worst heat of the day you might plan to start the party at 5 o'clock, play games until 6, have supper, then more games and a story session to round it off.

MENU

*Lemon-Grape Cooler
*Spaghetti and Meatball Casserole
*Banana-Coconut Logs on Lettuce
Bread Sticks
*"S'Mores"
Milk

RECIPES

LEMON-GRAPE COOLER

2 ingredients

YIELD: 20 4-ounce punch cups

2 3-ounce packages grape-flavored drink mix (I use Lipton
    Family Drink Mix.)
2 3-ounce packages lemon-flavored drink mix (I use Lipton
    Family Drink Mix.)

Method:
Early in the day:
1. Combine packages of grape mix with 4 cups water and freeze in
   ice trays.
2. Combine packages of lemon mix with 2 quarts (8 cups) water
   in large pitcher and chill in refrigerator.
3. To serve, place 2 or 3 grape ice cubes in each punch cup and fill
   glass with lemon drink.

SPAGHETTI AND MEATBALL CASSEROLE

4 ingredients

SERVES: 10

Equipment: 2½-quart casserole or baking dish

2 15¼-ounce cans spaghetti in tomato sauce with cheese
    (I use Franco-American.)
2 15-ounce cans meatballs in brown gravy (I use Chef
    Boy-ar-dee.)
5–6 slices mild cheddar cheese (or enough to cover)
1 8-ounce can tomato sauce with mushrooms (I use Hunt's
    Tomato Sauce.)

Method:
1. Combine the spaghetti and meatballs. Do this gently to avoid breaking up the meatballs.
2. Pour mixture into greased 2½-quart casserole or baking dish. (I use a 9- x 13-inch Pyrex one.)
3. Lay cheese slices over top.
4. Pour tomato sauce over the cheese.
5. Bake at 325°about 20–25 minutes, until bubbling hot. Cheese will melt and make a blanket over all.

BANANA-COCONUT LOGS ON LETTUCE

4 ingredients

SERVES : 10

    1 head lettuce
    5 ripe bananas
    ½ cup salad dressing (I use Miracle Whip.)
    1 cup shredded coconut

Method:
1. Slice lettuce finely and dry well in paper towels.
2. Cut bananas in half lengthwise and coat immediately with salad dressing. (A pastry brush is good for this.)
3. Sprinkle bananas generously with coconut. Store in refrigerator.
4. Serve on shredded lettuce.

"S'MORES"

3 ingredients

YIELD : 20 "sandwiches"

Equipment: barbecue or hibachi; long skewers or pointed sticks

    20 marshmallows
    40 square graham crackers
    20 chocolate mint patties

Method:

For each "sandwich":

1. Toast marshmallow on long skewer or pointed stick until light brown.
2. Place on graham cracker.
3. Place chocolate mint patty on marshmallow.
4. Top with another graham cracker and squeeze together gently. Taste. (Careful! They're hot!) Now you know why they are called "S'Mores."

TIPS FOR PREPARING AND SERVING Offer the children a drink of the Lemon-Grape Cooler as soon as they arrive. Also, have available a pitcher of ice water and paper cups.

"Dish up" in the kitchen, and set filled plates in front of each child at a patio table in the shade. Cookies and milk can be on the table for passing after children finish with main course.

A small barbecue or hibachi fire will be sufficient for the "S'Mores."

SETTING THE SCENE

Headquarters for the safari could be a tent set up under a shady tree. To make it look authentic, you could toss an inexpensive fishnet over the whole tent and wire small branches to the net. Folding camp stools are placed in a semi-circle at entrance to tent. The tree could be hung with long streamers made of green crepe paper to resemble hanging moss as found in the jungle.

For dinner, guests will sit at a folding camp-style table covered by a tarpaulin or a piece of camouflage material.

Make a big sign saying "Jungle Juice—Help Yourself" and prop it against a pail filled with frosty fruit juice or other punch. Place a dipper inside so that it can be ladled into paper cups. To make it seem more authentic, borrow or buy one of the long-playing records that imitate jungle birds so realistically. (I use Martin Denny's "Exotica" album.)

ENTERTAINMENT

Games are the most important part of any children's party. Here are some game suggestions for your jungle party guests.

OBSTACLE COURSE This is a good starter game to get everyone into an adventurous spirit. Explain that they are all on an African safari which is very dangerous and takes great courage. A sign will be found at each point with clear directions to the next obstacles. Players will run the course one at a time, and each will be clocked. The player to run the course in the shortest time will be known as "The Great White Hunter."

Sign at entrance to tent: "Safari Headquarters—Start here. Run to Banana Tree [any tree with 2 or 3 bananas hanging from a branch] and circle twice. Beware of python in tree [rubber snake]."

Sign at Banana Tree: "Cross suspension bridge [a ladder placed on ground, pointing to third obstacle] to Mountain Tunnel. Danger! Deep canyon below!"

Sign at Mountain Tunnel: "Crawl through to High Bridge. Warning! Lioness and cubs may be hiding in tunnel." (Tunnel may be made of kitchen chairs turned upside down and covered with a tarpaulin or blanket. Large cardboard cartons also make good tunnels.)

Sign at High Bridge: "Push forward at own risk to Pinnacle Point." (For bridge, lay a 12-foot piece of rope on ground. Player tries to walk on rope while looking through the wrong end of binoculars.)

Sign at Pinnacle Point: "Climb up and over and keep eyes peeled for Tropical Rain Forest." (Use 2 upright stepladders back to back.)

Sign at Tropical Rain Forest: "Proceed at full speed underneath the waterfall and head for the Snake Pit." (For waterfall, hang garden hose and sprinkler on fence.)

Sign at Snake Pit: "Jump across and get away from here fast. Look for Giraffe's Watering Place." (Snake pit is sand box with one rubber snake in it.)

Giraffe's Watering Place: "Take a drink and race to Safari Headquarters." (A pail of water is placed on top of ladder.)

As soon as one player returns, the next one is off.

SNAKE HUNT Pieces of string of various lengths have been hidden all over the backyard before the party. At the word "Go," all the players search for the pieces of string. At the end of 5 minutes they return to headquarters, and each one ties all his pieces of string together to determine who has the longest "snake."

JUNGLE QUIZ Here's a good one to play after supper. Maybe Dad will supervise. Two teams face one another as in a spelling bee. Dad gives the first question to the end man on the first team. If he misses it, the question goes to the end man on the second team. Questions are given first to one team, then the other. As soon as a player misses, he sits down. The game continues until one side is retired completely.

Questions and answers include the following:

> What animal is known as "King of the Beasts"? *(Lion)*
> Right or wrong: The elephant is the largest living land mammal. *(Right)*
> Right or wrong: Leopards are found in Africa and Asia. *(Right)*
> What kind of cry does a giraffe make? *(None)*
> What kind of noise does a lion make? *(Roar)*
> Right or wrong: Lions are carnivorous. *(Right)*
> Right or wrong: Zebras have red, white, and blue stripes. *(Wrong)*

Why are elephants' tusks valuable? *(Ivory)*

Right or wrong: Leopards hunt monkeys, birds, and reptiles for food. *(Right)*

Is the zebra more like a horse or a cow? *(Horse)*

Right or wrong: The leopard usually is yellow with black or brown spots. *(Right)*

Right or wrong: The elephant eats smaller animals. *(Wrong)*

Right or wrong: The elephant drinks water by sucking it into his trunk, then spraying it into his mouth. *(Right)*

What sound does a lion make when he's happy? *(Purr)*

Right or wrong: The python is a nonpoisonous snake. *(Right)*

Right or wrong: Hyenas have a soft, musical cry. *(Wrong)*

Right or wrong: A gazelle is a lady giraffe. *(Wrong)*

This list will give you the idea so that you can make up your own questions.

JUNGLE SCENE MURAL   Buy a roll of wide white shelf paper. Attach it to a fence or other flat surface. Place a big box of colored crayons or felt-tipped pens in a convenient spot and let guests paint a mural composed of large jungle plants, trees, flowers, ferns, animals, birds, anything they wish. Each is assigned a space of his own and each signs his masterpiece.

STORY TIME   No matter how familiar a story is, most of us enjoy hearing it again. Just before the party breaks up, gather together in a shady part of the garden and take turns reading one of the stories from *The Jungle Book, Dr. Dolittle,* or a Tarzan story.

Father's Day
Picnic in the Park

4:00 to 8:30 P.M.

Here's a gala picnic suitable for a club, business, or church group. Most cities have well-equipped picnic grounds in their parks, and for a group of any size, this makes the best location.

When choosing a site for a picnic, keep in mind the following conveniences: available drinking water; swimming facilities; shelter in case of rain (Heaven forbid!); rest rooms; barbecues or fireplaces, or a place where fires are permissible; grassy spots where you can stage contests and games. At many parks you can choose your location and make reservations for the number of barbecue grills you need.

A word of advice—rather than having an all-day affair, where everyone gets overtired, a short, sweet party is recommended. Better to get ready leisurely, plan on getting to the picnic site at 3:00 or 4:00, and leave around 8:30 when the campfire burns down.

Here is a good working schedule:

4:00 P.M.:	Assemble
4:30–5:30 P.M.:	Games and contests
5:30–6:30 P.M.:	Swimming
6:30–7:30 P.M.:	Supper and awarding of prizes
7:30–8:30 P.M.:	Campfire, group singing, ghost stories
8:30 P.M.:	Break camp and head for home

Good organization is necessary for everything to go smoothly. Here's one way to plan:

Two women make reservations and other arrangements at the park.

Four women plan picnic menu.

Two women take charge of decorations and table settings.

Two women plan games and contests and supervise them, with the help of several teenagers.

Two women head up a clean-up committee to guarantee that the park is left in good condition.

MENU

Pretzels and Beer   Pop for the Children
*Barbecued Cheeseburgers
Buttered Toasted Hamburger Buns
*Old-Fashioned Potato Salad
Corn on the Cob
*Strawberry Ripple Cake Squares   Homemade Peach Ice Cream
Coffee   Milk

RECIPES

BARBECUED CHEESEBURGERS

4 ingredients

SERVES: 12*

Equipment: large barbecue or 2 smaller hibachis; or oven broiler, if preparing at home

¼ pound margarine
1 tablespoon seasoned salt (I use Lawry's.)
3 pounds lean ground round steak (This is allowing ¼ pound per patty.)
6 slices cheddar cheese

*This amount of meat is easier to combine than the larger quantity; therefore, for 48, the recipe will have to be made up 4 times.

Method:

The day before:

1. Melt the margarine over low heat.
2. Add the seasoned salt to margarine.
3. Add margarine mixture to meat. Toss lightly.
4. Form meat into hamburger patties. Stack them, with waxed paper above and below each, or place each patty in a sandwich-size baggie. Refrigerate until picnic time.

At the park:

1. Build your fires at least an hour before barbecuing so that you will have a bed of glowing coals with a layer of gray ash on top. Rub an oil-saturated cloth over the grill to keep the food from sticking.
2. Barbecue hamburgers about one minute on each side for medium rare, slightly longer for well done. *Don't overcook*—meat continues to cook after it is removed from heat.
3. Place each on a well-buttered bun. Top each burger with one-half slice cheese. The hot meat will melt it just enough.

Note: For easier grill maintenance, line it with aluminum foil, then build your fire on top of it. This will not only make for easier cleaning, but the reflected heat will make your food cook more quickly.

OLD-FASHIONED POTATO SALAD

4 ingredients

SERVES : 50

Equipment: large salad bowls or air-tight plastic containers, such as Tupperware

16 pounds potatoes for boiling
 3 dozen eggs
 3 large bunches celery
 8 8-ounce bottles of Cole Slaw Dressing (I use Kraft.)
   Optional: 2 cups (1 pint) sweet pickles, chopped fine

Method:
1. Scrub potatoes, then boil in jackets until fork-tender.
2. Hard boil the eggs. Cool, then slice.
3. Clean, then dice celery.
4. Chill potatoes until cool enough to handle, then cut in ½-inch cubes into large container.
5. Add celery and sliced eggs while potatoes are still warm, and pour dressing over all. (This is the secret of good potato salad.) Mix very gently until dressing coats potatoes thoroughly.
6. Arrange chopped pickles over top if desired.
7. Refrigerate several hours or overnight.

STRAWBERRY RIPPLE CAKE SQUARES

4 ingredients

SERVES: 12

Equipment: 9- x 13-inch baking pan

1 14⅓-ounce package strawberry frosting mix (I use Pillsbury.)
2 3-ounce packages cream cheese (I use Philadelphia.)
2 eggs
1 18½-ounce package white cake mix (I use Pillsbury.)

Method:
1. Combine dry frosting mix with cream cheese in a large bowl.
2. Set aside, in small bowl, 1 cup of frosting to be used later for the top of cake.

3. Separate eggs. Beat egg yolks into the frosting mix in large bowl.
4. Prepare cake mix as directed on package, using remaining egg whites. Add 1 cup of cake batter to frosting mix in large bowl. Blend well.
5. Pour remaining cake batter into greased 9- x 13-inch cake pan.
6. Pour frosting mixture in large bowl over the batter, and with a table knife gently swirl the 2 mixtures together to get a pink and white, free-form, geometric effect.
7. Bake at 350° for 40–45 minutes, or until cake tester or toothpick comes out clean.
8. Cool completely in pan. Ice with frosting reserved in small bowl. Cut into squares.

Note: Sheet cakes such as this are very practical because they can be easily transported in the cake pan. Try to buy one with a close-fitting cover for this purpose.

TIPS FOR PREPARING AND SERVING   Four or five picnic tables will be necessary. Choose ones near the barbecue pits which you plan to use. If possible, serve children first, then clear the tables for the adults. Children can be kept amused and happy with a story session immediately following supper.

Even though it's a picnic, you can make the whole thing more festive by setting attractive tables.

Centerpieces of 3 or 4 white balloons are effective. These are also pretty hanging in nearby trees. Buy ones of good quality so they won't deflate, and before arranging them write sentiments such as: "We Love You, Dad"; "You're the Tops, Pops"; "Happy Father's Day"; "Dear Old Dad," etc. A wide felt pen is great for this.

Fitted, twin-size sheets are worth their weight in gold at any outdoor party. After you've set each table, cover it with a sheet to protect from insects, dust, and falling leaves. The fitted corners will secure the sheet over a 72-inch table.

ENTERTAINMENT

What makes a picnic memorable to young people? All these things have importance: anticipation, the drive to and from the picnic, swimming, the picnic supper. However, what really remains with us long after childhood is the memory of the games, the contests, the after-supper fun.

Most of all, it's the memory of lighting the campfire at dusk, the group singing in the firelight, the spooky ghost story session. Remember, adults enjoy ghost stories just as much as children, so bone up on the scariest ones you can find.

Some picnic games and contests are as much fun now as in Grandmother's day: Potato Race Relay, Horseshoe Contest, Three-Legged Race, Men's Nail-Driving Contest, and Tug of War.

A new one which can be very amusing is the Whistle Race. Men, women, boys, and girls all line up at the starting line, which is marked with a tape stretched between 2 rocks. Depending on the amount of space available, decide on a finish line.

The games chairman explains that when he blows the whistle, everyone will start racing toward the finish line. However, when he blows the whistle again, everybody must turn around and run the other way. This occurs several times and each time players must reverse. First one over the finish line wins—and it could well be the little three-year-old child. This is fun both for the participants and the audience.

This baseball game to end all baseball games will probably be the highlight of the day. It's Handicap Baseball and it's Mothers versus Fathers. At first everyone will think, "Why, that's no contest. The Fathers will beat the Mothers all hollow!" But there's a catch to it. The Fathers have to pitch and catch with the opposite hand—right handers having to use the left hand, and vice versa. In addition, Fathers have to run backward between bases. The last time we played, the Pops still beat the Moms— but not by much. The score was 30 to 27. The only tough decision was for the kids: whether to root for Mom or for Pop.

WATER BALLOON CONTEST Husband-wife teams compete in this contest. Husbands line up side by side, about 3 feet behind the starting line. Wives stand in a line facing them, also 3 feet behind the line. Each husband is given a blown-up balloon which contains about ¼ cup of water. (Put the water in first, then blow up balloon and tie a knot in end.)

The starter yells "Go" and each husband tosses balloon to his wife. The starter then says, "Everyone step back one pace." The wife tosses the balloon back to her husband. The game continues in this way, everyone stepping back a pace each time. Players are disqualified if they fail to catch the balloon or if a balloon breaks. Last couple left wins. The kids will want to try this too, so bring plenty of balloons.

BUBBLE GUM CONTEST FOR THE KIDS Contestants are lined up facing the spectators. A piece of wrapped bubble gum is given to each. At the word "Go," each unwraps the gum and starts to chew it. The first to succeed in blowing a bubble wins.

FOLLOW THE LEADER Adults as well as children will enjoy this version.

The leader starts off with all the players lined up behind him. They must do as he does. Each time he shouts "Change," he adds one more action, but he always goes through all the preceding steps. Here's an example:

1. Step forward 1–2–3 hop, 1–2–3 hop, etc. Repeat until he yells "Change."

2. 1–2–3 hop, flap arms up and down in flying motion. Repeat until leader yells "Change."
3. 1–2–3 hop, flap arms, now say "Cock-a-doodle-doo."
4. Repeat first actions, add "Run around the nearest tree."
5. Repeat first actions, act like an Indian by looking to left and right while shading eyes.

To vary the actions, the leader might walk pigeontoed; do a Charlie Chaplin shuffle with feet pointing out; make an Indian war cry; walk with knees bent and arms swinging like an ape. As a grand finale, leader runs completely around group with everyone following in a circle. By this time everyone will need a rest!

Fourth of July
Reunion Supper

FOR 24

6:00 to 9:00 P.M.

We all look forward to special holidays, particularly when we have nice long weekends. One of the most exciting holidays is the Fourth of July, with parades, exhilarating martial music, flying flags, and fireworks displays. This year why not plan a bang-up family reunion, back in your own backyard, with everyone from 3 to 93 included?

All will go much smoother if it's well organized. No one person should try to take all the responsibility. A good idea is to get the women together a week or two in advance so that all may have a hand in the preparations. One could coordinate the menu so that each family would contribute a certain food item. One could offer to oversee serving the food and washing up afterward. One could take charge of "setting the scene"—decorations, table settings, and placement of outdoor furniture.

Another important department is games and contests. The person in charge of this has the job of planning entertainment which will appeal to all age groups—some active games for the youngsters, somewhat quieter ones for adults, and some in which everyone can participate.

MENU

Potluck parties, where each family contributes an item or two of food, are an excellent idea when a large number of people are involved. One easy way is to ask half the women to bring a favorite

102 ❧ *Summer Parties*

salad and the remainder to bring a favorite dessert. The host and hostess supply the main course, rolls, and coffee.

Remember that the menu will be completely different each time you follow this method.

*Chicken Breasts, Thighs, and Legs Oven-Glazed
in Barbecue Sauce
Salads:
*Three-Bean Salad
*Cabbage and Green Grape Slaw
*Macaroni Salad
Tossed Greens with Creamy Roquefort Dressing
*Oven-Browned Sesame Toast Fingers
Desserts:
*Caramel-Coconut Layer Cake
Chocolate Nut Torte
Apple Pie with Cheese
Frosted Cup Cakes
Soft Drinks   Milk   Coffee

RECIPES

CHICKEN BREASTS, THIGHS, AND LEGS OVEN-GLAZED IN BARBECUE SAUCE

3 ingredients

SERVES: 24 (2 pieces each)

Equipment: electric roaster or large oven roaster

12 whole chicken breasts
12 legs and thighs
 1 18-ounce bottle barbecue sauce (I use Kraft.)
 4 tablespoons chicken-flavored stock base (I use Schillings, which comes in a jar in paste form.)

Method:

1. Cut chicken breasts in half. Cut legs and thighs in half. Your meat man will usually do it for you.
2. Arrange a layer of chicken pieces in roaster.
3. Stir chicken-flavored stock into ½ cup of barbecue sauce. When blended, combine with remainder of sauce.
4. Pour about ½ cup of the sauce over the layer of chicken.
5. Arrange another layer of chicken and cover with sauce.
6. Continue in this way until all chicken and sauce have been used.
7. Cover and roast at 350° for about one hour, basting occasionally with the sauce. Chicken should be fork-tender and slightly brown. Serve very hot.

Note: I always use an electric roaster for any number over **16**. It makes for carefree cooking, particularly out of doors. If dinner is delayed, temperature may be turned down to 200° and heat will be maintained automatically.

THREE-BEAN SALAD

4 ingredients

SERVES: 24 generously

3 16-ounce cans cut green beans, or 3 15-ounce cans garbanzo beans
3 16-ounce cans cut wax beans
3 16-ounce cans kidney beans
3 8-ounce bottles Italian dressing (I use Bernstein.)

Method:

1. Drain all beans in a colander. (Reserve juices, if you wish, for soup pot.)
2. Pour beans into large, covered container.
3. Pour Italian dressing over beans and marinate several hours or overnight.
4. Toss lightly again just before serving.

CABBAGE AND GREEN GRAPE SLAW

3 ingredients

SERVES : 8

Equipment: wooden chopping bowl; vegetable chopper

1 medium head cabbage (This will make about 8 cups finely grated cabbage.)
1 8-ounce bottle cole slaw dressing (I use Kraft.)
2 cans white grapes or 2 cups fresh seedless green grapes

Method:
1. Toss together the cabbage and dressing.
2. Carefully mix in grapes.
3. Cover container and store several hours, or until thoroughly chilled, in refrigerator.

MACARONI SALAD

4 ingredients

SERVES : 6 to 8

$\frac{1}{2}$ pound elbow macaroni (approximately 4 cups)
2–3 stalks celery (1$\frac{1}{2}$ cups diced)
1 cup slivered or diced American cheese
1 cup bottled Thousand Island dressing
Salt and pepper to taste

Method:
1. Cook macaroni according to directions on package, usually 8–10 minutes or to the al dente stage (just tender).
2. Toss all ingredients together. Season to taste.
3. Store in refrigerator until well chilled.

OVEN-BROWNED SESAME TOAST FINGERS

4 ingredients

YIELD : 72

Equipment: cookie sheet

- 2 2⅛-ounce packages whole sesame seeds
- 8 tablespoons dried minced onions
- ½ pound butter
- 1 24-ounce loaf white bread, regular slices (approximately 18 slices

Method:
1. Pour sesame seeds into pie plate and toast in preheated 400° oven until golden brown, about 8 minutes.
2. Pour minced onion and sesame seeds into paper bag and shake well.
3. Melt butter in pie tin.
4. Remove crusts from bread slices and slice into 4 pieces lengthwise.
5. Dip each piece into melted butter, then shake in bag with minced onion and toasted sesame seeds.
6. Place each piece separately on cookie sheet.
7. Bake in 400° over for 8–10 minutes until toast is golden brown. These are especially good warm.

CARAMEL-COCONUT LAYER CAKE

4 ingredients

SERVES : 10

Equipment: 3 layer-cake pans; 1 flat cake plate or silver tray

- 1 package caramel cake mix (I use Duncan Hines.)
- 2 cups shredded coconut
- 1 pint heavy cream, for whipping
- 1 cup brown sugar

Method:

1. Bake cake according to directions on package in 3 layer-cake pans.
2. Place on racks to cool.
3. Spread the coconut on cookie sheet and brown in the oven at 350°. Watch carefully and remove from oven as soon as it gets a light golden brown.
4. Whip the cream and add the brown sugar.
5. Spread between layers and on top.
6. Sprinkle toasted coconut on top.

TIPS FOR PREPARING AND SERVING   Put your electrical equipment to work! If you have an electric roaster, set it on a patio table early in the day, all ready to be plugged in later on for roasting the chicken.

Here's one way of serving the food and beverages:

Sink bottles and cans of soft drinks in crushed ice in a large tub to keep frosty cold.

Make coffee well ahead of time. A large 30-cup electric coffee pot is a *must* for a crowd. Set out sugar and cream just before serving.

Host serves chicken as guests file by with their plates.

Set bowls of salad in slightly larger bowls, half filled with crushed ice.

Keep Toast Fingers hot in electric bun warmer or electric frying pan on lowest setting.

Arrange desserts on 2 shelves of serving cart for a beautiful display.

SETTING THE SCENE

Setting the scene is always an important consideration in planning a successful party, and it is just as important to provide comfort at an outdoor party as at an indoor one.

Furniture can be arranged in cozy, conversational groups, with tables nearby for glasses, ashtrays, sunglasses, etc. Seating should be provided for everyone—not necessarily chairs for all, but benches, floor cushions, etc. Comfortable patio chairs will be needed for elderly guests.

There should be some shady areas; if shade trees are not available, you might consider making a canopy out of gay and inexpensive print or striped yard goods. Denim is particularly serviceable.

Lawn umbrellas provide a festive look. Six-foot Japanese sun umbrellas are widely available at reasonable prices.

An open fire after dark always contributes excitement and glamor, particularly to children. Modern fire pits are perfect for this, or you can use an outdoor barbecue or even a portable one.

After-party litter can be avoided by placing trash baskets in convenient locations and by supplying plenty of ashtrays, preferably deep ones so that the wind can't scatter the ashes. Tin cans sprayed black or a bright color, half filled with sand, or small flower pots make dandy outdoor ashtrays.

One hostess turns the clean-up process into a game. She has a box full of small surprises for the children—these to be distributed as soon as all pieces of paper or other litter are deposited in proper containers. Prizes are modest—balloons, lollypops, whistles, and the like. Children work like beavers to earn them.

You can make inexpensive placemats for picnic tables by covering 9- x 13-inch pieces of cardboard or poster boards with blue foil gift wrap, which can be bought by the roll. Use red, white, and blue paper napkins and white paper plates. Two or three Uncle Sam top hats act as centerpieces.

An alternate idea is to cover pieces of cardboard with red and white striped giftwrap paper. Either staple or glue them together. Good quality paper napkins can be used in solid blue, or use two napkins folded together, one in blue, one in white.

For more formal indoor parties, red, white, and blue flowers make an eye-catching centerpiece. Although you can usually find red and white flowers, it isn't always possible to find blue ones. To get around this problem, you may have to use blue in some other way, such as the following:

Flag-blue tablecloth; red, white, and blue striped napkins made of yard goods; white china; milkglass goblets; red carnations and white chrysanthemums in a footed milkglass compote for a centerpiece.

Red, white, and blue striped tablecloth made of yard goods; white napkins; blue-rimmed white ironstone dishes; flag-blue goblets. For a centerpiece, use a circle of flags secured in a styrofoam ring with a pair of tall white candles at each end.

ENTERTAINMENT

Excellent books on games are available at almost every public library, so the Contest and Game Chairman will have no trouble finding a variety.

Here is one that small children love.

RAINBOW SCRAMBLE   Buy a package of 9- x 12-inch construction paper in an assortment of colors. A different colored sheet is used for each child. Cut each sheet into 100 or more pieces. A simple way is to mark the sheet into 1-inch squares, 12 squares down and 9 squares across, to make a total of 108. Cut 3 or 4 sheets at one time into 1-inch squares. Mix the squares all together in a large bowl.

Each child is given a small paper bag on which a paper square is pinned or stapled. He must only collect paper squares in his color. At the word "Go," the leader throws all the little squares into the air, all over the backyard. The hunt is on! As children gather them, they put them into the little bag. They are allowed a maximum of 10 minutes. First one to gather all of his squares wins the game.

(Don't worry about being a litterbug. They'll search until they find all the pieces.)

TIN PAN BAND Sometimes known as the Tin Pan Band, other times as the Kitchen Orchestra, this is one form of entertainment which is hard to beat. It is particularly appropriate for the Fourth of July, because everyone can get into the act and make as much noise as he wishes. Don't overlook that 93-year-old! He or she may have a better sense of rhythm than anyone else.

Collect as many noisemakers as you possibly can. Here's a list of the ones we use:

> a toy drum
> dry beans in a glass jar (Have several of these available.)
> toy washboard and a stick or stiff brush
> pot lids to bang together as cymbals
> kazoos (lots of these)
> toy xylophones
> slide whistles
> jingle bells on a ribbon
> several tambourines
> mouth organs
> toy horns
> maracas
> bongo drums

Under ideal circumstances you will have a pianist, guitarist, or accordionist who will bang out the tunes. In the absence of live music, however, your Tin Pan Band can successfully accompany records or even singalongs. The main idea is that everyone can participate.

> Favorite numbers for the Tin Pan Band are:
>
> "The Stars and Stripes Forever"
> "When the Saints Come Marching In"
> "Darktown Strutters Ball"
> "Beer Barrel Polka"
> "Won't You Come Home, Bill Bailey"
> "Happy Days Are Here Again"
> "Bicycle Built for Two"

"I'm Looking Over a Four-Leaf Clover"
"Marine's Hymn"
"Sailing, Sailing"
"Anchors Aweigh"
"Air Force Song"
"The Caissons Go Rolling Along"
"Put on Your Old Gray Bonnet"
"Deep in the Heart of Texas"
"Tea for Two"
"There Is a Tavern in the Town"
"Yankee Doodle Dandy"
"California, Here I Come"

Well, you get the idea—all the wonderful old songs which have a strong beat.

BANG!! "Bang" is similar to "Pin the Tail on the Donkey." Attach a line of blown-up balloons to a fence. Paint an X on half of them with nail polish. The object of the game is to try to stick a pin into the ones marked with an X.

As in the old game, a player is blindfolded, then given a pin, turned around 3 times, then pointed in the direction of the balloons. Whoever breaks the most balloons marked with an X wins the prize. (Let the children take over the job of blowing up the balloons.)

Allow about 5 balloons per player. There is plenty of fun and suspense for both player and spectator.

Garden Wedding and Reception

FOR 35

8 :00 to 9 :30 P.M.

Customs are changing. Much of the stiff, formal procedure is being by-passed by modern brides in favor of a simpler, more meaningful home wedding, shared by relatives and close friends only. It can be just as sacred, just as beautiful in every way. Best of all, it eliminates the tension of rushing from one location to another.

Portions of the ceremony itself are often written by the young couple, expressing what marriage means to them.

In place of organ music, often only the sweet strains of a guitar or harp can be heard.

It is the combination of traditional customs and individual touches that makes the modern marriage ceremony more personal and significant. Despite the departure from ritual, young people usually wish to incorporate some of the ''good old customs,'' and ask questions such as ''When do we cut the cake? How is it done? When is the toast proposed? Who does it? How is it worded? What does the bridegroom say in response?''

With this in mind, it might be helpful to describe a particular wedding which we found very appealing.

That loveliest, most poignant hour, twilight, was selected.

Early-arriving guests strolled in the flower-scented garden prior to the ceremony, stopping on the way to sign the bride's book, which was presided over by two younger sisters.

A tiny summerhouse across one corner of the garden provided an enchanting background for the ceremony. As the hour approached, guests lined the lawn area leading to the summerhouse. This had been decorated with green branches and white flowers and gave the appearance of a chancel. The minister, two bridesmaids, and the best man took their places in front of it, facing the guests.

The theme song of ''Love Story'' was played softly on the

guitar as the bride and groom walked slowly, hand in hand, along the garden path leading to the outdoor chancel.

The bridesmaids took their places beside the bride and the best man stepped into position beside the bridegroom. Parents of each stood nearby, slightly closer than guests.

The ceremony was simple and lovely, and at its conclusion, after the kiss, members of the wedding party and parents embraced the couple. Guests then came forward to talk to the young couple and wish them happiness.

Leisurely, guests and the wedding party strolled to the covered terrace which had been chosen for the reception.

Trays filled with cups of punch were passed. Guests had their choice of champagne punch or a frosty fruit drink. White and silver cocktail napkins were also on the tray.

When all of the guests had spoken to the couple, the best man asked for attention, then made the toast to the bride, with everyone except the bride and groom drinking with him. The bridegroom responded by thanking his best man and telling the guests how happy they were to have them there.

Guests were then invited to the buffet table, which was placed against one wall of the patio. Dainty sandwiches, a dessert-type salad, petit fours, nuts, mints, and coffee made a satisfying mid-evening supper.

After this course, guests were directed to the wedding cake table where the young couple posed for pictures. The bridegroom placed his right hand over the right hand of his bride. Then together they cut the first slice of cake from the bottom tier. A silver cake knife, decorated with white satin ribbons, was used. The bride and groom followed the custom of sharing this first piece of cake, symbolizing their shared life together in the future. A close friend of the family then cut and served wedding cake to the guests, carefully keeping the decorated top tier intact.

Just before leaving to change into street clothes, the bride assembled her unmarried friends, then ascended a few stairs, turned away from the girls, and threw her bridal bouquet over her shoulder. It is said that she who catches the bouquet will be the next bride!

The couple made a special point of bidding good-bye quietly to each of the parents—thanking them again—then were off amid expressions of good luck and happiness.

A wedding such as this is a great deal easier to plan and carry out than a large formal affair. In addition, expenses are much lower. Certainly, everyone concerned will be more serene, and in most cases happier. It could be the answer to the wedding coming up in your family.

Many families can't afford an extravagant occasion. Here are a few suggestions which may be of help to the bride.

There are many costumes available now which include a well-cut, pretty cocktail-type dress and coat of the same length. They are especially handsome in winter white wool or in one of the autumn shades—pumpkin, russet, gold. Wear the dress for the wedding, then don coat, hat, and gloves to convert to a going-away outfit.

Instead of an expensive bridal bouquet, carry a prayer book, on which may be pinned an orchid in colors to harmonize with your costume. Later, pin the orchid to one shoulder of your coat.

Use flowers from the garden to supplement greens and flowers ordered from the florist.

Limit your guest list to family and closest friends. Most homes won't hold more than 25 or 30 comfortably.

Help your mother send handwritten invitations. Maybe she could write the actual invitation and you could address envelopes, put on stamps, and return address stickers. (If your home is hard to find, it's a kindness to enclose a map and/or directions.)

Don't say no to offers of assistance. Almost every woman loves to help with a wedding. Friends and relatives can arrange flowers, help with the cooking, arrange the tables, assist with the wedding cake, run errands, help with the serving.

Decide on nonalcoholic punch instead of champagne—or serve a champagne punch if you're on a tight budget.

Plan a late afternoon or early evening wedding so that a simple menu will be sufficient.

MENU

Champagne Punch   Frosty Fruit Juice
Open-Faced Sandwiches   *One-Bite Chicken Rolls
*Frosted Lemon Petit Fours   Decorated Cookies
*Homemade Mints   Salted Nuts
Wedding Cake
Coffee

RECIPES

ONE-BITE CHICKEN ROLLS

4 ingredients

YIELD : 6 dozen

Equipment: cookie sheet or small-cup muffin tins

3 8-ounce packages refrigerated layered dinner rolls (I use Pillsbury Butterflake Dinner Rolls.)
12 large ripe olives, pitted
3 cans delicatessen-style chicken salad spread (I use Swift's Deli-Spred.)
1 3½-ounce package sliced almonds

Method:
1. Remove dinner rolls from package. You'll notice that there are about 6 *very thin* layers in each roll. Instead of baking the whole rolls as would ordinarily be done, separate each roll into 3 pieces of dough, each composed of 2 layers.
2. Fold each piece of dough in half and pinch edge (as you would in Parker House rolls). Place on cookie sheet. Bake at 375° for 12–14 minutes or until golden brown.
3. Cut olives into small pieces.
4. Combine chicken salad spread, sliced almonds, and diced olives.
5. Split rolls just far enough open to stuff with 1 teaspoon chicken salad spread. Press slightly to hold together.

Note: These may be made ahead except for filling, which should be made shortly before serving. Other delicious sandwich fillings are crabmeat, shrimp, lobster, tuna, and ham salad.

FROSTED LEMON PETIT FOURS

4 ingredients

YIELD : 6 dozen

Equipment: extra-small-cup muffin tins, measuring about 1¾ inches across

1 18½-ounce box white cake mix
2 eggs (as called for in recipe on package)
1-pound box confectioner's sugar
1 tablespoon lemon extract
   Optional: A few drops of yellow food coloring for the frosting

Method:

1. Make up cake mix according to directions on package.
2. Grease well small muffin tins. Put 1 rounded teaspoon batter into each cup.
3. Bake approximately 15 minutes at 350°, or until light brown. Cool.
4. Make up frosting, a little at a time, by adding a few drops of flavoring and a few drops of hot water to confectioner's sugar. The mixture should pour slowly, about like thick honey.
5. Place tiny cakes upside down on an oven rack placed over a shallow pan. Dribble icing from a spoon held above the cakes. Move in circles so that the icing flows down all sides and completely covers cakes. (Excess icing which flows off into pan may be scooped up and used again.)
6. Let frosting dry until firm before transferring to serving plate. Use a pancake turner for this.
7. Well-washed, fresh flowers tucked around outer edge of plate give a pretty effect.

HOMEMADE MINTS

3 ingredients

YIELD : about 80

4 ounces (½ large package) cream cheese (I use Philadel-
    phia.)
1 teaspoon peppermint flavoring
1-pound box plus 1 cup confectioner's sugar

Method:

1. Bring cheese to room temperature.
2. Add peppermint. Mix in sugar, first with a fork, then with
    hands. Knead until like pie dough, adding more sugar if sticky.
3. Roll into balls about the size of a marble. Place on wax paper.
4. Flatten with back of fork. Allow to harden before serving.

TIPS FOR PREPARING AND SERVING   For the Champagne
Punch, you'll need a punch bowl, punch cups, ladle, tray, and
cocktail napkins. An easy, efficient way of serving is to fill 6 or 7
punch cups, place them on a tray along with napkins, and pass to
guests. This eliminates a bottleneck around the punch bowl. Ask
someone to be in charge of punch bowl.

Open-Faced sandwiches, One-Bite Chicken Rolls, Petit Fours
and Cookies may all be arranged on trays or footed cake plates
and placed on table. A stack of salad-size plates should be centered
on each side of table. Guests serve themselves.

Arrange mints and nuts on serving plates or in candy dishes
and place on table. Place a small spoon in each.

For the coffee service, you'll need a silver or china coffee pot,
cream pitchers, sugar bowls, spoons. When guests have selected
the "goodies" they prefer, the relative or friend pouring coffee
will set the filled cup right on the plate. This makes it easier for
the guest than trying to juggle a cup and saucer with one hand
and a plate with the other.

Center the wedding cake on a separate round table.

SETTING THE SCENE

FOR AN OUTDOOR WEDDING

Because every garden is different, it's necessary to design your own "stage set," as it were. I believe you'll find it a help to sketch it on paper first.

Here are the main considerations:

Where will the ceremony take place?

By what route will the bride and her attendants arrive at the altar area? To protect shoes and gowns it's preferable to follow a path.

Where will the buffet table be set up? It should be as near the kitchen as possible for ease of serving.

How many guests can circulate comfortably in the area available? Remember that every guest at a home wedding stays on for the reception.

Do you have some lawn chairs or benches where elderly guests may be seated? A pretty lawn umbrella and a few pieces of garden furniture will add a lot to the charm of your setting.

Many gardens have a spot which is just a "natural" as a background for the ceremony. Here are some examples: a wishing well; a rustic garden gate entwined with rambling roses; a lily pool, fountain, or small waterfall; a spreading old tree; two blooming rose trees with space between; a large flowering vine against a wall or fence (wisteria is breathtaking); two trees spaced at least 10 feet apart; a corner rock garden.

If you have none of these things, one of the following ideas may be helpful in designing an altar area.

Put up a garden trellis in the center of a green hedge. Decorate it with white flowers and greens. (Trellises are inexpensive and are usually available at nurseries and hardware stores and through mail order catalogues.)

Put up a pair of trellises in a corner of the garden, one on one wall and one on the other. A standing basket of flowers, greens, and ferns on each side would be pretty.

In many modern homes, the patio is almost enclosed by the house. In that case, plan the altar area against a wall. A rope of greens secured to a central support, then caught up at the sides before cascading to the ground, would give the illusion of an arbor. A semi-circle of evergreens in pots or potted flowering plants will add a gay note.

A chicken-wire frame is often used as a support on which to wire or staple greens and flowers. It would have to be at least 7 feet square to be effective.

I strongly recommend using a separate table for the wedding cake. It dramatizes the cake much more if it can reign in solitary splendor rather than be crowded on a buffet table with other food items. It looks particularly enchanting placed in the center of a round table.

One of those round table tops, about 48 inches across, placed on a card table works perfectly. Cover with a dainty round cloth, preferably of lace or flocked organdy.

The cake may be encircled with ferns and fresh flowers.

Nearby, place a stack of small white paper plates and napkins and a row of dessert forks.

Paper plates and napkins of excellent quality are now available. Clear plastic forks and spoons look very pretty and are inexpensive. They are being used even at elaborate weddings.

The bride's cake traditionally is cut with a beribboned silver wedding cake knife, often engraved with the initials of the bride and bridegroom and the wedding date. Its companion piece, the silver cake server, is used both for serving and for removing the top tier of the wedding cake, customarily saved for the couple's first anniversary.

FOR AN INDOOR WEDDING

When choosing the site of the altar area, take into consideration the way in which your rooms are designed. Everyone will want to be able to watch the ceremony, so give this careful thought. Some possibilities are in front of a tastefully decorated fireplace; in front of a picture window (if at night, draperies could be drawn); the corner of a room, which makes a nice background when decorated.

One wedding which stands out in my mind was especially pretty. A bower of greens formed the background. Two white latticed rose trellises were set up in a corner, one on one wall, the other at right angles to it. A profusion of trailing ivy was wired to the trellises. Fresh white carnations and pale yellow gladiolus florets were tucked into the greens. These flowers were chosen because they remain fresh out of water. Tall baskets of white and yellow flowers stood on each side.

An archway between rooms is often a good choice as guests in either room get an unobstructed view. Cathedral candelabra entwined with ivy and tiny flowers add an important note. Candles should be tall and white for best effect.

These spots all lend themselves well to decoration:

Out-of-doors, at each side of door, place matching pots of plants in bloom.

In the entry hall a wreath of jewel-toned fruit with a tall candle in the center is handsome on a low table.

Long pieces of ivy, arranged in a copper bowl, are pretty on a fireplace mantel. Arrange them so that they are entwined across the mantel and cascade down at either end. Substitute spring blossoms or autumn leaves depending on the season.

At harvest time, a tall floor vase with various golden-hued grains—rye, barley, oats, and sheaves of wheat—is appropriate.

In the powder room put a small blooming plant (pink begonias or African Violets are pretty) or a tiny mixed bouquet of fresh flowers.

For an evening wedding, use lots of lighted candles in halls, living room, and dining room. Candlelight casts a romantic glow over everything and creates a party atmosphere much more than harsh overhead lights do.

ENTERTAINMENT

Music lends enchantment to any party, but at no time is it more desirable than at a wedding.

Friends who play a musical instrument well are usually glad to oblige. If this isn't feasible, you might consider engaging a small combo. Their charges are often surprisingly reasonable. Otherwise, gay, light music on your record player adds to the festive atmosphere.

Of course you'll want pictures. Either arrange for a commercial photographer or have a friend substitute. Supply him with plenty of film and flash bulbs or cubes.

On a table put the wedding book. Assign one of the younger members of the family to take charge and to make sure that each guest signs it.

TOASTS Toasts to the bride vary greatly in content and length, and no two people express themselves in exactly the same way. I've heard toasts which lasted as long as five minutes while others took only a few seconds. A sincere, complimentary remark first about the bride, then the groom, followed by wishes for their future happiness, is in good taste and adds to the joyous spirit of the reception.

Midsummer Tropical Luau

Hula maids casting a magic spell,
Tall cold drinks from a pineapple shell,
Dreamy music of soft guitars,
Midsummer madness beneath the stars.
Pale gold moon from out of the East
Will light your way to an island feast
In our own little garden, to be precise,
Turned into a tropical paradise.

A tropical luau must take the prize for being the prettiest and most romantic of all parties.

An intriguing invitation can set the scene for a festive party far in advance and stimulate excited anticipation. Very pretty note paper is available now. Choose one featuring bright colored flowers.

Suggested schedule:

7:00 P.M.:	Punch is served
8:00 P.M.:	Buffet supper
9:00–10:30 P.M.:	Games, dancing, and sing-along
10:30–11:00 P.M.:	''Farewell to Thee''

MENU

The next item is planning the menu. When Hawaiians give an authentic luau, whole porkers are roasted on large revolving spits or baked in a pit. Whole suckling pigs are difficult to obtain, however, so this isn't too practical here. Recently, people have roasted delicious pork loins on electric rotisseries which can be plugged in outdoors, enabling guests to enjoy the heavenly fragrance.

ISLAND FEAST

Mai Tai Punch Bowl
*Fresh Fruit Kabobs in a Watermelon Boat
Boneless Center-Cut Roast Loins of Pork (cooked on rotisserie)
Stuffed Baked Yams   *Green Goddess Salad
Sesame Bread Sticks
*Rainbow Coconut Ice Cream Balls   Coffee

RECIPES

FRESH FRUIT KABOBS IN A WATERMELON BOAT

4 ingredients

SERVES: 18

Equipment: wooden skewers, 2 or 3 for each guest

  1 large watermelon
4–6 cups fresh strawberries with stems left on, or fresh Bing
     cherries
  1 fresh pineapple, cut into bite-sized chunks
  1 large cantaloupe

Method:

1. Cut off a thin slice from one side of watermelon. This is to make it stand evenly.
2. On top side cut off about a third. Make scallop or zigzag design around the top of watermelon.
3. Scoop out watermelon balls from the bottom and lower sides. Set aside and keep refrigerated.
4. Scoop out cantaloupe balls.
5. Wash strawberries or cherries.
6. When assembling kabobs try for good color contrast, something like this—first a cherry, then a cantaloupe ball, then a cube of pineapple, then a watermelon ball; then start over again until wooden skewer is filled.
7. Arrange skewers by sticking ends into watermelon boat.

Midsummer Tropical Luau   🎋   *123*

GREEN GODDESS SALAD

4 ingredients

SERVES: 18

Equipment: large salad bowl

- 4 quarts lettuce, romaine, or fresh spinach, in bite-sized pieces
- 4 cups shrimp, cooked and cleaned
- 6–8 medium-ripe tomatoes
- 1 cup Green Goddess Dressing

Method:
1. Dry greens carefully between paper towels and store in refrigerator.
2. Cut shrimp into bite-sized pieces.
3. Cut each tomato into 8 wedges.
4. Toss greens and shrimp with dressing in large bowl at serving time. Garnish with tomato wedges.

RAINBOW COCONUT ICE CREAM BALLS

4 ingredients

SERVES: 18

Equipment: paper cups, small muffin tins, wax paper

- 1½ gallons vanilla ice cream
- 2 4-ounce cans finely shredded coconut (I use Baker's Southern Style Coconut.)
- 1 box food coloring, various colors
- 18 flat-bottomed ice cream cones

Method:

1. Pack ice cream into small muffin tins.
2. Place in freezer until solid.
3. Have ready 3 cupfuls of tinted coconut.*
4. Pour each color onto square of waxed paper.
5. Remove ice cream balls one at a time and roll in tinted coconut and immediately return to muffin tin.
6. Cover each muffin tin with Baggie and store in freezer.
7. Place flat-bottomed cones on tray. Place an ice cream ball in each cone. Pass tray of cones to guests.

   * To tint coconut: In each of 3 bowls stir a drop or two of food coloring into 1 teaspoon water or milk. Add 1 cup shredded coconut to each. Stir until coconut is colored evenly. Recommended colors: pale pink, pale yellow, pale green.

TIPS FOR PREPARING AND SERVING Place Mai Tai Punch Bowl on sturdy table which has been covered with a floral print cloth. Have punch cups and cocktail napkins nearby.

Put Fresh Fruit Kabobs on long platter or tray. Place on buffet table.

Set Roast Loins of Pork on buffet table. Host carves between ribs and serves one to each guest.

Turn back foil on Stuffed Baked Yams just as you are ready to serve. Arrange in large wicker baskets.

Place salad tongs in bowl of Green Goddess Salad; guests serve themselves.

Stand Sesame Bread Sticks upright in heavy goblet or tumbler.

Remove Rainbow Coconut Ice Cream Balls from freezer 10 minutes before serving. Place one in each cone.

SETTING THE SCENE

An appropriate location could be a family room, garden, shipboard, church social hall, beach house, or recreation hall.

To add to the atmosphere, choose from these suggestions:

Plenty of greens in large vases, bowls, or wicker cages suspended from the ceiling or wall brackets.

Fish netting attached to ceilings, falling in graceful folds.

Flowers, shells, leis, fish cutouts attached to the netting.

Tiki torches flickering in the far corners of the garden.*

Hurricane lamps on tables, shelves, and window ledges.

Candles in glass jars placed at the bottoms of trees and in among bushes.

Japanese lanterns strung in trees or terrace. (Use long-burning votive candles.)

Christmas lights in green and blue.

Traditionally, guests at a luau sit on the ground and eat from a very low table. However, this becomes uncomfortable when one is not used to it. An idea which I like very much is to set 3 long tables in a U-shape.

The table in the center is used for your buffet, and the other two tables are used for seating. In this way, guests can easily go back for seconds if they wish.

Here are some suggestions for table coverings:

Bamboo roll-up shades come in a variety of sizes and colors. When placed on a table top they give an Oriental feeling. For strong color, you might use a lime green shade, then for contrast, bamboo placemats in shocking pink and/or purple. If you have trouble finding shades in the color you want, spray paint them. It only takes a minute or two.

* Tiki torches have various names and are often called Luau torches. Kerosene is poured into a metal container, then attached to top of a 6-foot pole. A wick protrudes through the top. This is lighted and gives a dramatic effect for hours.

Yard goods departments now have an abundance of tropical prints in wild colors. You'll need 6 yards to make a 72- x 108-inch tablecloth.

Fish nets in many bright colors can be found in luau kits, variety stores, and mail order catalogues. These are effective placed over sheets or tablecloths to give a nautical feeling. One great advantage is that you can pin or tie other decorations to the net, such as small sea shells, cork floats, plastic lobsters, miniature sea horses, etc.

The punch bowl is especially eye-catching when the base is encircled with green ivy, among which is placed fresh blossoms.

Attractive plastic drinking glasses are available in the shape of a pineapple for a nominal sum. Or use inexpensive plastic glasses, possibly in pale pink.

The following are some centerpiece suggestions:

An abundance of fresh fruit is most appropriate and authentic looking. Lay fresh green leaves down the center of a long table in a serpentine pattern. Arrange peaches, plums, pears, apples, oranges, etc., following the design. When in season, fresh cherries, tucked here and there, give brilliant color.

Pineapples, of course, come to mind first when we think of the islands. I sometimes make fruit arrangements in a pair of wooden compotes which are about 5 inches high. I place a fresh pineapple in the center of each, then 2 pears in opposite corners, and 2 peaches in the remaining corners. For the second layer I use smaller fruits such as cherries, apricots, and plums. Two or three varieties of grapes, cascading over the sides, complete the picture. It takes only a few minutes and is very pretty.

Another easy way to decorate for a banquet is with a row of fresh pineapples spaced about every three feet. A small paper lei in vivid colors draped casually over each gives a pretty effect. If you wish, fill spaces in between with sprigs of green leaves.

ENTERTAINMENT

SOUTH SEAS TREASURE HUNT   The hostess can make an announcement something like this : "I have a surprise for you and a *big* prize for the winners. [The big prize was a *big* watermelon.] We're all going on a South Seas Treasure Hunt."

Hand each couple an entry blank like this :

You are now on a hunt for the articles listed below. They are all in plain sight. Some of the articles are the real thing; others are pictures. As you find the various articles, write the location in the space opposite.

The couple who locates the greatest number of articles wins first prize. Time limit is 15 minutes.

Ready, Set, Go!

Fish net
Cork float
Sea shells
Raffia hat
Paper lei
Driftwood
Banana
Life preserver
Hurricane lamp
Wicker basket
Coconut
A tropical flower [This can be an artificial orchid, hibiscus, or bird of paradise.]
A tropical bird [These are artificial ones usually found in the dime store.]
Cruise ship [magazine picture]
A tree house [This is a small bird house.]

And so on. List about 20 articles if you can.

Note: Have the Treasure Hunt as soon as all guests are assembled so as to get the party off to a merry start. Another good time is right after dinner, to keep up the momentum of the party.

The lovely, haunting strains of Hawaiian music contribute more to establishing an authentic atmosphere than anything else. There are countless Hawaiian records from which to choose.

If someone plays the guitar or other musical instruments, it would be lovely to have a sing-along. Here are a few of the best-loved Hawaiian melodies:

> "Aloha"
> "To You, Sweetheart, Aloha"
> "Hawaiian Wedding Song"
> "My Little Grass Shack"
> "Lovely Hula Hands"
> "Blue Hawaii"
> "Sweet Leilani"
> "Song of Old Hawaii"
> "Drifting and Dreaming"
> "Hawaiian War Chant"
> "Kalua"
> "Across the Reef"
> "Pagan Love Song"
> "Song of the Islands"

Autumn
Parties

The Bachelor
Entertains at Lunch

FOR 8

Saturday, 12:30 to 4:00 P.M.

Here's a good way for a bachelor to entertain without too much work or confusion. Have the gang over to view the big football game together—or the Kentucky Derby, or the New Year's Tournament of Roses Parade, or perhaps election returns. There are any number of television shows of universal interest, which are more enjoyable when shared with a group of friends.

No need to fret about fancy table settings or a complicated menu—and certainly there's no need to worry about how to entertain the guests!

When extending invitations, specify casual dress—pants suits, sweaters and skirts for the women, sport shirts and slacks for the men.

MENU

Take-out food is widely available, surprisingly inexpensive, and comes in many varieties in cities of any size.

It isn't necessary to order in advance at the majority of hamburger places or shops specializing in take-home chicken dinners, but it's usually advisable to special order a day or two in advance from restaurants.

What will it be? Chinese Chow? Dutch Lunch? Italian Spaghetti and Meat Balls? Hot Pastrami Sandwiches from the delicatessen? Mexican food?

HOME-COOKED LUNCH

Fritos   Pretzels   Salted Nuts
Beer

*Roast Filet of Beef Sandwiches
Packaged Onion Rings or Potato Chips
Pickles   Olives
*Date-Filled Oatmeal Cookies
Coffee   Tea

RECIPES

ROAST FILET OF BEEF SANDWICHES

4 ingredients

SERVES: 8–10

Equipment: roasting pan; meat thermometer

1 4–6-pound beef tenderloin*
1 8-ounce bottle Italian Dressing
½ pound butter
2 loaves fresh sandwich bread, thinly sliced

    * A tenderloin roast is the same as filet mignon, but it is all cut in one piece. Ask the butcher to choose one as uniform as possible, since you will be using it for sandwiches. Sometimes these roasts are inclined to be large at one end and small at the other. If he doesn't have one large piece, buy two that weigh 2–3 pounds. It's fairly expensive per pound, but there is very little waste and it's deliciously tender.

Method:
1. Marinate the roast for several hours in Italian dressing.
2. Preheat oven to 325°.
3. Insert a meat thermometer and roast the beef for about 50 minutes, or until thermometer registers 140° for rare, 150° for medium rare, or 160° for medium.
4. Remove from oven. Let rest 10–15 minutes. This rest makes for easier carving and juicer meat.

Note: I prefer these sandwiches with just salt and pepper, but if you wish you could have a choice of toppings such as a pungent mustard sauce, a sour cream and horseradish sauce, and, possibly, chutney.

   The roast beef sandwiches make a substantial snack to follow cocktails, or you can make a satisfactory supper by adding a casserole of scalloped potatoes, salad, and a simple dessert.

DATE-FILLED OATMEAL COOKIES

3 ingredients

YIELD: 2 dozen

Equipment: cookie sheet

1 13-ounce package oatmeal cookie mix (I use Nestle's.)
1 egg, as called for on package
2 cups pitted dates

Method:
Cookies:
1. Preheat oven to 375°.
2. Beat the egg with 4 teaspoons water.
3. Combine cookie mix and egg mixture.
4. Drop by level teaspoons on ungreased cookie sheet.
5. Bake 10–12 minutes at 375°, until light brown at edges. Cool.

Filling:

6. Cut up dates. Add 1 cup water.
7. Cook dates and water approximately 5 minutes or until thick, about the consistency of jam. Remove from heat.
8. Spread date mixture generously on flat side of a cookie, then cover with another cookie, keeping flat sides together.

Note: These are exceptionally delicious cookies which keep well. Other thick jam fillings may be used in place of dates.

TIPS FOR PREPARING AND SERVING Ready-Prepared Food: In advance, clear off a table near the television. Set a stack of paper plates, napkins, salts, peppers. and silverware on a tray nearby.

Invite friends to serve themselves as soon as the food arrives, to enjoy while it's piping hot. Guests sit where they please, probably the majority on floor cushions close to the set.

A large coffeemaker, preferably the 30-cup size, could be plugged in in the same room. To protect furniture and carpeting, set it on a tray. Nearby stack hot drink cups, cream, and sugar. Guests serve themselves whenever ready throughout the day.

Home-Cooked Lunch: Place snacks in bowls on various tables.

Sink cans of beer in chipped ice in large bowl. Place cocktail napkins nearby. Invite guests to help themselves.

For roast beef sandwiches, place roast in oven about 1 hour before serving time. Slice the roast in very thin slices and pile generously between slices of hot buttered bread. Mmm! Everyone selects his own seasonings.

Set out sandwich ''go-withs'' (packaged onion rings, potato chips, pickles, olives) in bowls near the roast beef.

Arrange dessert on plate beforehand, and set out after guests finish sandwiches.

Coffee should be available from the time the party starts.

SETTING THE SCENE

There are some great albums featuring college marches. The sound of a band blaring as guests enter is stimulating and gives promise of fun to come. Look for albums that include familiar tunes like "On Wisconsin," "Notre Dame Victory March," "Far Above Cayuga's Waters," "Fight on for U.S.C.," "Navy Blue and Gold," and "The Stein Song," just to name a few.

Here are a few suggestions for decorations you might consider. For class reunions, for instance:

Enlargements of class pictures, particularly graduating classes.

Cluster of balloons, with Class of '60, or whatever, marked in large letters with a felt pen.

Pennants from the high school or college.

For a large class reunion, have classmates and spouses autograph a felt table runner. The runner needn't be anything fancy—just a piece of light-colored felt, approximately 15 inches wide and 72 inches long, pinked around the edges. Have guests write with a wide-nibbed felt pen in large letters. To be effective, each signature should be about 12 inches long, and should be written at various haphazard angles. This makes a nice memento and may be added to at subsequent reunions.

ENTERTAINMENT

Consider forming a football pool to add spice to the game. Here's one simple way to conduct a pool:

Host writes numbers from 0 to 48 on a piece of paper, then cuts slips apart so that each one is separate. He places them in a bowl or hat, well mixed up.

Each player antes 25¢ or 50¢ or $1, whatever is decided on. If there are 8 players, each would take 6 slips. The winning number is the combined score of both teams.

Cocktails and Buffet Supper

This may sound odd, but it's true—sometimes it's less work and easier on the nerves to entertain a large number of guests than just a few. The main reason for this is that 20 or more guests are bound to entertain one another with little help from the host or hostess. What group of this size could possibly get together without a conversational hum—or, more likely, a roar? There's nothing dearer to a hostess's heart than a hubbub of conversation, laughter, and music.

Guests lists have a way of growing, what with house guests of your own and house guests of guests being included. For many years when I found myself making a long list, I'd decide regretfully, ''Well, I guess it will have to be the same old 6 :00 to 8 :00 cocktail party.''

Then I'd start to dread all those hard-to-make, hard-to-keep-fresh, cocktail tidbits. A person never knows whether they will all be eaten up in the first 15 minutes, or whether they will be ignored and still be there the next morning. Sometimes it goes one way, sometimes another. What worried me the most is that guests go away hungry. Canapés don't satisfy the majority of people and they usually have to stop for dinner on the way home or raid the icebox after they get there.

The majority of cocktail invitations specify 5 :30 to 7 :30, or 6 :00 to 8 :00. Most dinner party invitations say 7 :00 or 7 :30 to ?. I like a party that is somewhere in between—a little longer than the conventional cocktail party, yet shorter than the dinner party, which can go on far into the night.

Here's a party suitable for celebrating a birthday, entertaining out-of-town friends, or welcoming a new neighbor, to name a few possibilities.

6 :00 P.M. : Guests arrive
6 :00 to 7 :30 P.M. : Cocktails and snacks
7 :30 to 8 :30 P.M. : Buffet supper
Approximately 9 :00 to 9 :30 P.M. : Guests leave

This makes for a short and sweet party with a simple but satis-fying supper. The menu need not be elaborate—a main dish, a salad, hot rolls, and coffee. If you serve dessert, make it a very simple one.

MENU

Martinis Manhattans Daiquiris Bloody Marys *Apple Punch
Nibblers
*Turkey Noodle Bake
Mixed Greens with *Garlic Roquefort Salad Dressing
*Blueberry-Lemon Molded Salad
Cornbread Sticks
Assorted Cookies   Coffee

RECIPES

APPLE PUNCH

4 ingredients

YIELD : 20 punch cup servings

Equipment: punch bowl

3 3-ounce packages raspberry gelatin
8 cups (2 quarts) apple juice
½ cup lemon juice
1 30-ounce bottle ginger ale

Method:
1. Dissolve gelatin in 2 cups boiling water. Add 2 cups cold water.
2. Add apple and lemon juices and ginger ale.
3. Pour into punch bowl. Add ice.

Note: The flavored gelatin adds color and flavor to the punch.

TURKEY NOODLE BAKE

4 ingredients

SERVES : 25

Equipment: large cooking pot or Dutch oven roasting pan

- 1 3-pound (approximately) boned and rolled frozen turkey roast
- 5 10½-ounce cans condensed cream of chicken soup (I use Campbell's.)
- 3 8-ounce packages fine noodles
- 5 10-ounce packages mixed frozen vegetables (I use Birdseye Japanese-style vegetables.), or green peas and pearl onions

Method:
The day before the party :
1. Remove cellophane bag from frozen turkey, but do not remove the net bag in which it is wrapped.
2. Place turkey in large kettle or Dutch oven. Add 2½ quarts (10 cups) water. Cover. Simmer for about 4 hours or until fork-tender. Turn turkey roll over once or twice during that time so that it will cook evenly.
3. Cool quickly and refrigerate, covered, until ready to use.
4. Remove turkey from broth. Reserve broth. Cut turkey into bite-sized pieces, about the size of a walnut. You'll find that this is an easy job, as there are no bones, just solid meat. You'll need 20 cups. A half-gallon measure comes in handy here.
5. Measure 2 quarts (8 cups) turkey broth into the same large Dutch oven. Combine with the undiluted cream of chicken soup, a little at a time for smoothness. Add turkey pieces.

6. Cook noodles in 4 quarts (16 cups) boiling water. Follow directions on package, cooking until *just* tender, known as the *al dente* stage. It usually takes 8–10 minutes. (To avoid having spaghetti, noodles, or macaroni boil over, add a tablespoon or two of salad or olive oil to the boiling water.)
7. Drain carefully, preferably through a colander. Run water over noodles to keep them separated. Pour into greased roasting pan.
8. Cook mixed vegetables according to directions on package. Be very careful not to overcook. Fold gently into turkey mixture.
9. Add turkey mixture to noodles in roasting pan. You'll have to use your hands to mix thoroughly without breaking up the noodles. Add salt and pepper to taste. Refrigerate overnight.

The day of the party :
10. Reheat in 325° oven for 1½ hours or until bubbling hot.

GARLIC ROQUEFORT SALAD DRESSING

4 ingredients

YIELD : 3½ cups (approximately)

Equipment: blender

   1 8-ounce bottle oil and vinegar dressing (I use Kraft.)
   ½ package Italian salad dressing mix (I use Schilling.)
   2 3-ounce packages Roquefort cheese
   1 pint dairy sour cream

Method:
1. Whir ingredients together in blender.
2. Serve with mixed greens for a salad ; use as a dip for raw vegetables, such as celery or carrot sticks, scallions, or cauliflower buds ; use as a sauce with steak, lamb chops, or ground round patties.

BLUEBERRY-LEMON MOLDED SALAD

3 ingredients

SERVES : 12

Equipment: 9- x 13-inch glass casserole

1 6-ounce package lemon gelatin
2 14½-ounce cans blueberries
1 pint dairy sour cream (to be used as topping)
   Optional: Lettuce for garnish

Method:
1. Soften gelatin in ½ cup blueberry juice.
2. Heat blueberries until simmering. Add softened gelatin. Remove from heat.
3. Pour mixture into casserole. Place in refrigerator several hours or overnight. (May be made 2 or 3 days in advance.)
4. Cut into 12 sections. Place on tray and garnish with lettuce if desired.
5. Spoon a tablespoon of sour cream in center of each piece, or place a bowl of sour cream near the salad and have guests serve themselves.

TIPS FOR PREPARING AND SERVING   The self-service cocktail party has several things to recommend it :

It permits the host and hostess to welcome friends at the door and visit with them during the evening.

It keeps the guests circulating.

By having drinks in various locations, you're not likely to have a bottleneck in any one spot.

Here's how to set up your "Easy-on-the-Host" Cocktail Party:

The night before the party, make up a pitcherful each of Martinis, Manhattans, Daiquiris, Bloody Marys, and Apple Punch. Store in refrigerator. Place in covered bowls the garnishes which go with each:

> For the Martinis: stuffed olives or small pickled onions
> For the Manhattans: Maraschino cherries
> For the Daiquiris: thin lime slices
> For the Bloody Marys: lemon wedges
> For the Apple Punch: orange slices, cut in two
> (If you really want to be ready, have each impaled on a round, white, smooth pick.)

An hour before the party, half fill 5 large bowls with crushed or chipped ice. Make a little hollow in the center of each bowl. Place a pitcher in the center of each. (The pitcher will be warmer than the ice and will sink in, making a little "nest.")

Set each bowl in a different location. One might be on a coffee table, one on a hutch cabinet, one on a long shelf, one on a serving table.

Take a piece of construction paper. Fold in half lengthwise and write or print with a felt pen, Daiquiris, or Martinis, or whatever. At each location have on hand cocktail napkins and the proper garnish. Guests are invited to serve themselves. (Men usually serve cocktails to their dates, but sometimes they forget!)

A supper such as I've described, which follows cocktails, can be served very informally. Unless a person has a very large home, it's not practical to seat this many guests at a table. The simplest way is to place the food on a table, possibly in the dining room in the wintertime or on a patio table outdoors in the summertime, and invite guests to serve themselves. They are then free to find a chair, floor cushions, or whatever.

Many modern homes have a raised hearth, which is great for additional seating. Ours is 27 inches wide and 9 feet long. We covered long foam cushions in a durable, tweedy fabric and have found it tremendously practical for parties. It provides comfortable seating for 6 people.

SETTING THE SCENE

An all-candlelight party is a beautiful thing which creates an instant festive atmosphere. Use lighted candles on the buffet table, in wall sconces, on mantels, or grouped on a large coffee table. A polyglot mixture of candlesticks, holding candles of various colors and heights, placed close together is surprisingly effective.

Fresh chrysanthemums and fall leaves, arranged in scooped-out pumpkins or eggplants, are nice touches at this time of year.

Hostesses often make the mistake of moving out most of the furniture to make more room. This gives a cold, unlived-in appearance. Guests enjoy sitting down occasionally and visiting in small conversational groups. Try to keep your guest list pared down to a reasonable number. You'll find that you, as well as your guests, will have a better time.

Hobo Supper for Halloween

7:00 to 11:00 P.M.

There are few parties more fun than a Hobo Party. Costumes, of course, are a must! This particular party was written for the "Young Marrieds," but is suitable for other age groups as well.

The ideal location would be a cabin in the woods, but a recreation room, family room, or decorated garage will do nicely.

An amusing invitation piques the curiosity and promises fun. Write them on torn pieces of brown paper with a black felt marking pen. Head the invitation something like this:

WHAT?	A Hobo Party
WHO?	The McCroskeys
WHERE?	Hobo Heaven, 4321 Main St.
WHY?	To celebrate Halloween
WHEN?	Oct. 31st at 7 o'clock

Nobody gits in that's clean 'n purty
Gen-u-wine hoboes is mean 'n dirty
Whoever shows up most tattered 'n torn
Will win the prize—a jug of corn ! ! !

(The prize will be just that—a bottle filled with black and orange candy corn.)

MENU

*Frosty Harvest Moon Punch
*Texas Jailhouse Stew
Baked Spuds   Toasted Onion Rings
*Crisp Vegetable Sticks to Dunk
*Hunks of Hot Buttered Bread
*Tiny Fried Apple Pies
Java

RECIPES

FROSTY HARVEST MOON PUNCH

4 ingredients

YIELD : 32 punch cups

1 fifth vodka
3 1-pint cans frozen orange juice
1 large 28-ounce bottle sparkling soda
1 pint pineapple sherbet

Method:
1. Pour vodka into punch bowl.
2. Add orange juice undiluted. (The crushed ice dilutes sufficiently.)
3. At serving time add 2–3 quarts crushed ice.
4. Add soda water and top with sherbet.
5. Stir gently and serve.

TEXAS JAILHOUSE STEW

4 ingredients

SERVES : 16

Equipment: Dutch oven; 2 large kettles

4 pounds round steak
1⅔-ounce package stew seasoning mix (I use Lawry's.)
6 10½-ounce cans brown mushroom gravy
4 20-ounce packages frozen stew vegetables

Method:

1. Remove most of the fat and gristle, if any, from round steak. Cut meat into 1-inch cubes.
2. Brown meat over medium heat in heavy Teflon-lined Dutch oven.
3. Add seasoning mixed with 2 cups water. Pour over meat. Turn heat down to simmer and cook for 2½-3 hours or until meat is very tender.
4. Pour mushroom gravy over meat.
5. Cook vegetables in 2 large kettles according to package instructions.
6. Combine meat and vegetables just before serving.

CRISP VEGETABLE STICKS TO DUNK

4 ingredients

SERVES: 16 (about 1 quart)

8 medium carrots
2 whole hearts of celery (approximately 16 stalks)
2 8-ounce packages cream cheese (I use Philadelphia.)
2 8-ounce cans green chili sauce (I use Ortega brand, Green Chili Salsa.)

Method:

1. Clean vegetables early in the day and cut carrots and celery into long, narrow strips. Store in cold water in refrigerator. Pint jars are good for this, and for this Hobo party, you can simply drain the water off at serving time and put one of the jars between each two guests.
2. Allow the cream cheese to come to room temperature, then beat slowly with electric beater until creamy. Add the chili sauce and beat until well combined. It will be a delicate pink color and oh, so delicious. Keep refrigerated until serving time.
3. If possible place 1 jar of vegetables and 1 bowl of dip between each two guests. (Nice clean tuna cans make an appropriate container for dip.)

HUNKS OF HOT BUTTERED BREAD

3 ingredients

SERVES: 16

Equipment: cookie sheet

1 pound butter or margarine
2 teaspoons garlic salt, or 2 cloves garlic
2 large loaves unsliced bread

Method:
1. Melt butter.
2. Add garlic salt to butter and combine well. (If you prefer using fresh garlic, put the 2 cloves through a garlic press or cut up very fine.)
3. Tear bread apart in uneven hunks about the size of lemons.
4. Dip chunks in melted butter, place on cookie sheet, and heat in hot oven, 450°, for 5 minutes.

TINY FRIED APPLE PIES

4 ingredients

YIELD: 8 small pies

Equipment: electric frying pan

1 9½-ounce package pie-crust mix
1 cup canned apple-pie filling (I use Comstock or Wilderness.)
2 cups homogenized shortening (I use Crisco.)
¼ cup granulated sugar (for topping)

Note: For 16, make recipe twice. It's easier to work with the smaller amount. You will not need additional shortening; there is enough left in the frying pan for a second batch.

Method:
1. Pour pie-crust mix in small bowl. Add 4 tablespoons cold water.
2. Mix with fork a few seconds until it forms a ball. Roll ball in hands a few seconds until it is firm and smooth.
3. Cut into 16 wedges. The easy way to do this is to cut ball in half with sharp knife. Turn and cut in half the other way so that there are 4 wedges. Cut each in 4 portions.
4. Remove one of the small wedges, roll into a ball, then roll into a 3-inch circle on floured board. For accuracy, use a cookie cutter or jar top. Set aside. Follow the same procedure for a second one.
5. Place 1 teaspoon apple-pie filling on a pastry round. Cover with another pastry round. Press the edges of the two rounds together with a fork all the way around so that the filling is sealed within.
6. Measure shortening into electric frying pan and set at 380°.
7. Continue making the remaining pies.
8. When the temperature of the shortening reaches 380°, place about 4 of the small pies in the frying pan. Fry about 3 minutes until edges turn light brown.
9. Turn the pies gently, using two slotted spoons or egg turners so that the grease will not be disturbed. Fry another 2–3 minutes until golden brown.
10. Remove to tray on which you've placed a double thickness of paper towels.
11. Turn pies over when cool enough to handle, so that rounded side is up. Sprinkle with granulated sugar.

For maximum flavor, reheat a minute or two in low oven just before serving.

Note: These pies are quite small. If your guests have large appetites, you may need more than one per person. You'll find that they are really delicious.

TIPS FOR PREPARING AND SERVING Guests line up in the kitchen and are served right from the range, where the stew can be kept good and hot. (Set the large, heavy pot in simmering water in an open frying pan which is just a little larger in diameter. In this way the stew remains hot without danger of burning.)

Arrange the rest of your spread on the kitchen table and let everyone help himself.

Set vegetable sticks and bowl of dip between each 2 guests.

After the main course, gather up the plates and remaining food and whisk them off to the kitchen.

Pass the Tiny Fried Pies on a tin plate; guests eat them out of hand. (Anything goes for starving hoboes.)

SETTING THE SCENE

When we think of hoboes we think of trains and railroad yards. Large signs can be made up bearing the names of railroads; also signs such as "Beware—Railroad Crossing" or "Stop, Look, and Listen." Letter other large signs such as schedules of arrivals and departures on a bulletin board. Maybe you could even rig up a standing crossing signal such as you see out in the country. Put up signs saying "Hobo Jungle"; "No Smoking, Offenders Will Be Prosecuted"; "No Tramps Allowed—This Means You ! ! !"; "No Loitering." Outside, over the front door, have the admonition: "Tramps Use Back Door." These signs are easy to do when you have a thick felt pen. Use posterboard or even art paper.

If you can get small photos of some of your guests, mount them on pieces of art paper with large black "Wanted" signs above the photos. Write description of crimes underneath. You can get some ideas from the lobby of the post office.

You can obtain a spooky effect by using green or blue bulbs in lamps. You might cover windows with black paper or gunnysacking.

For tables, use long planks over sawhorses. Cover these with several thicknesses of newspapers.

For napkins, buy red and white bandannas from the dime store. Bandanna prints are also available in paper napkins.

Tin plates are used for the stew and vegetables; nice clean tuna cans for the dip; tin cups for java.

ENTERTAINMENT

SING-ALONG   Hope that you have a guitarist, accordionist, or pianist in the group. Here are some good songs for a Sing-along:

> "Hallelujah, I'm a Bum"
> "The Prisoner's Song" ("If I Had the Wings of an Angel")
> "King of the Road"
> "Birmingham Jail" (the tune is "Down in the Valley")
> "Casey Jones"
> "Atchison, Topeka, and the Santa Fe"
> "Blues in the Night"
> "Don't Fence Me In"
> "Happy Days Are Here Again"
> "I Got Plenty of Nothin' "
> "Lazy Bones"
> "Nature Boy"
> "Sentimental Journey"

RAILROAD BINGO   Hearing the names of some of these railroads will strike a nostalgic note with many of you.

Write the names of 16 railroads on a large piece of paper. Cut them apart and put the 16 slips into an old hat.

Give each guest paper and pencil. Ask guests to divide the sheet of paper into 16 squares. (Mark 3 lines across the page at equal distances and 3 lines up and down.)

Hostess draws a slip from the hat and calls out the name, say, Canadian Pacific Railway. Each player writes it in one of the 16 squares (any square). Just use initials—CPR. Possibly the next slip drawn is Great Northern. She calls it out and everyone writes that one in a square. And so it goes until all names have been called. Players should have all the squares filled. (Understand that each player's entry sheet will be different.)

The hostess now throws all the slips back into the hat and mixes them well. She repeats the performance of drawing out one slip at a time. This time the player crosses off the railroad as she calls it. The first player to get 4 across, 4 up and down, or 4 vertically wins the prize.

Here is a list of well-known railroads: Canadian Pacific; Grand Trunk; Southern Pacific; Baltimore and Ohio; Atchison, Topeka, and the Santa Fe; Great Northern; Pennsylvania; Chesapeake and Ohio; Illinois Central; Lehigh Valley; New York Central; Union Pacific; Wabash; Burlington; Chicago Great Western.

BROOM DANCE   Couples start dancing. An extra man or girl is given a broom for a partner. When the man sees a girl he wants to dance with, he taps her partner and that man has to dance with the broom. And so it goes with the broom changing hands every few seconds. If you have an equal number of men and girls, you can use two brooms—one for the men to dance with and one for the girls.

BALLOON SWEEP RELAY (men vs. girls)   You will need 2 brooms and 2 balloons (one black, one orange). This game is a lively one and lots of fun, especially adapted for a church or club recreation hall.

Four men line up, one behind the other, at one end of the room. The other 4 line up opposite them at the other end of the room.

The girls follow the same procedure. The first man and the first girl in line are each given a broom and a blown-up balloon. (Additional balloons should be available in case some break.)

At the signal, each places the balloon on the floor, then starts sweeping it to the other end of the room, cheered on by his team-mates. The brooms pass to the next in line and that person begins to sweep it back to the other end.

The team who uses short, accurate strokes is more likely to win. Those who get excited and use too hard a swing will probably either break the balloon or find it sailing through the air into left field somewhere.

Thanksgiving Dinner

Harvest home, Harvest home,
We have plowed, we have sowed;
We have reaped, we have mowed;
We have brought home every load;
Hip, hip, hip, Harvest home!

These are the words of an old English song, sung in thanksgiving that the crops had all been safely brought in and that plentiful food was assured for another year.

A village festival was held in the village church. The master or squire sat down and shared the feast with all the other members of the parish—the farmers, their families, the tradespeople; in fact, everyone in the village was invited and each brought armloads of vegetables, fruit, and other provender which was piled high in glowing array at the front of the chapel.

It is thought that memories of these festivals influenced the Pilgrims in their wish for a similar celebration in America.

With most of us doing our entertaining without benefit of household help, it's necessary to use as many shortcuts and modern conveniences as possible. I find the boneless turkey one of the greatest of these. It can be placed in the oven solidly frozen at 3:25 and removed from the oven at 5:30, brown and tender and ready to carve in beautiful, even slices as soon as the gravy is made.

With the exception of the turkey and gravy, every single thing may be made the day before.

MENU

Ice Cold Celery Sticks   Ripe Olives
*Roast Boneless Turkeys   *Baked Stuffing Balls Amandine
Cranberry Sherbet
*Souffléed Potatoes   Brown Gravy
Candied Yams   Creamed Onions
Pumpkin Tarts   Frosted Grapes   Spicy Sugared Nuts
Coffee   Milk

RECIPES

ROAST BONELESS TURKEYS

SERVES: 16

2 40-ounce frozen turkey roasts, seasoned and boned (I use
Checkerboard with pan and giblet gravy packet.)

Method:

1. Do not defrost. Preheat oven to 425°.
2. Remove roasts from boxes and discard pan lids. Fold foil
   lengthwise and tent them lightly over roasts.
3. Cook 1 hour and 30 minutes. Remove foil tents and cook 35
   minutes longer to internal temperature of 175°.
4. Remove from pans. Let stand 10 minutes before slicing. (Total
   cooking time 2 hours, 5 minutes.)
5. To make gravy, add boiling water to contents of gravy packets
   and cook as directed.

Note: Each turkey roast provides 8 ¾-inch slices or 24 ¼-inch
slices.

BAKED STUFFING BALLS AMANDINE

3 ingredients

YIELD : 32

Equipment: 4 medium 8-cup muffin tins

4 7-ounce packages herb-seasoned stuffing mix (I use Kellogg's Croutettes.)
4 10 ½-ounce cans cream of chicken soup
2 cups slivered almonds

Method:
1. Toss ingredients lightly together. Let stand at room temperature about 30 minutes.
2. Press handful of mixture lightly into a ball. (Add a little boiling water if it doesn't hold its shape.) Place each stuffing ball into a greased cup of muffin tin. Set aside until ready to bake.
3. Bake at 350° for 45 minutes until crisp and golden brown.

SOUFFLÉED POTATOES

4 ingredients

SERVES : 16

Equipment: 9- x 13-inch baking dish

1 7-ounce package instant mashed potatoes (I use Betty Crocker Potato Buds.)
4 egg whites
1 pint sour cream
1 cup grated Parmesan cheese

Method:

Early in the day:

1. Bring 1 quart of water and 1 tablespoon salt to a boil in large pot. Remove from heat.
2. Stir in potato buds, whipping with fork until desired consistency. If potatoes are too thick, add a little more water.
3. Beat egg whites until stiff. Fold into hot mashed potatoes.
4. Arrange in greased baking dish.
5. Dot potatoes with sour cream.
6. Sprinkle Parmesan cheese evenly over top. Set aside.
7. Reheat potatoes for 15 minutes in 350° oven. They can be reheated after you remove the turkey to "rest."

TIPS FOR PREPARING AND SERVING   Store celery sticks and ripe olives in refrigerator until serving time.

The Roast Turkey is carved in the kitchen by the host, then slices are kept hot in a saucepan set in a large frying pan half filled with simmering water. The turkey stays hot and moist. While the host carves the turkey, the hostess makes gravy.

Store cranberry sherbet in freezer until serving time.

Stuffing Balls, Souffléed Potatoes, Candied Yams, and Creamed Onions have all been made the day before and stored in casseroles in refrigerator. They are all reheated in medium oven for 30–40 minutes or until bubbling hot.

Arrange pumpkin tarts on a serving tray on buffet in dining room with plates and forks nearby.

Frosted Grapes and Spicy Sugared Nuts are served later in the evening.

SETTING THE SCENE

This is one of those occasions when all the best table linen is pressed, china and glassware polished, and silverware shined.

Here are a few suggestions for table centerpieces:

One or two cornucopias, sometimes called horns of plenty, lavishly spilling freshly washed vegetables, is particularly appropriate at Thanksgiving. Fill in open spots with nuts in the shell. Cornucopias are available in glass, wicker, metal, wood, or papier mâché. Arrange candles at random in uneven lengths for an interesting effect.

Six or eight glass candlesticks from the ten-cent store grouped together give an imposing effect to your holiday table. They may be arranged in a circle around a floral centerpiece or the bases disguised with autumn leaves and small flowers such as pompon chrysanthemums. You may group three together at each end of your centerpiece, using 15-inch, 12-inch, and 10-inch candles.

Another idea is to arrange a line of eight candlesticks, the two tallest in the center, the rest diminishing in size. Arrange fruit around the bases.

A dessert centerpiece is sure to draw compliments. Arrange pumpkin and/or chess tarts on a footed cake plate, then tuck pompon chrysanthemums of various colors into the vacant spots. These particular flowers keep fresh for several hours out of water.

For another idea, arrange a fresh fruit platter, possibly apples, oranges, bananas, pears, grapes. Tuck wedges of Saran-wrapped cheese here and there—crackers, too, if you wish. Have small plates and fruit knives ready. Many guests prefer fresh fruit and/or cheese to heavy desserts after a rich dinner.

Chrysanthemums, in various sizes and colors, arranged in a scooped-out pumpkin, make a festive spot of color in the living room. An easy way is to pack a heavy flower container full of short sprigs of greens—whatever you have on hand. Fill the bowl with water, then arrange your flowers. Leave fairly long stems on them. The tightly packed sprigs hold each flower stem securely. Set the whole arrangement into the scooped-out pumpkin.

ENTERTAINMENT

GOBBLE GOBBLE Here's a game guaranteed to convulse the 7- to 12-year-old set, particularly after they've been tricked and are able to watch the others. Children usually get more fun out of a game if some of the adults participate too. Hope you have some good sports at your house!

Either buy a cardboard turkey at the ten-cent store, or draw one with a good long beak. Tape it to the wall or a door. It is explained to contestants that they are about to play a game similar to "Pin the Tail on the Donkey." However, in this game, they are simply to point with their right forefinger to the beak of the turkey, then walk forward, while blindfolded, and see who can come closest to touching the beak. Two or three contestants are given a trial run so that everyone understands. All the contestants are requested to leave the room. One is called back, blindfolded and, with an arm outstretched, is guided toward the turkey's beak. Just as the exploring finger is about to touch the picture, it is given a decided bite. This is accomplished by means of a clothespin or kitchen tongs.

I predict that boys as well as girls will let out a shriek as they are called in one by one and are unexpectedly "bitten" by the turkey.

ALL I WANT FOR THANKSGIVING Here's a round-the-table game which will appeal to most age groups.

Mother gives each player 10 beans or chips. She starts the game by saying, "All I want for Thanksgiving are some apples." The next person names an edible item beginning with the letter *B*, the next with *C*, and so on.

When a player misses, he forfeits a bean and the next person in line tries. Play becomes increasingly difficult as the alphabet is repeated, for a different food item must be announced each time. Play continues until one person has all the beans, which won't take too long, as you'll find out. It's best to eliminate the really difficult letters such as *I, J, K, Q, U, V, X, Y,* and *Z*.

Nothing tickles a child's fancy more than adults entering wholeheartedly into games with them. However, it's no fun if adults do this with a tongue-in-cheek attitude or a patronizing manner. To be really fun for children, adults must get into the spirit of the thing and really try to win.

Here's a slightly different version; it's called "Count Your Blessings."

At the party where I learned this game, the guest of honor was asked to start the game with a word beginning with the letter *A*. He said, "I'm grateful for affection." Thirteen-year-old Susie giggled and said, "I'm grateful for boys."

The hostess said, "I'm grateful for children." Bobby, 9 years old, said, "I'm grateful for dumplings," and so on to the end of the alphabet.

The more ridiculous the word, the more fun it is. If the game is going well, you may want to go through the alphabet two or three times. Of course, you may never repeat a word.

Theater Supper
for Senior Citizens

FOR 8

6:00 to 8:30 P.M., CURTAIN TIME

Theater parties are enjoying a popular revival due to the increasing interest in live theater. Road companies from New York are playing to sell-out houses in almost all large cities. Many large- and medium-sized cities boast their own symphony orchestras, little theater under the stars, chorale groups, dance companies, barber shop quartets, ballet companies, high-school and college drama groups.

In addition to these organized groups, many clubs and churches put on annual programs, so there are many occasions for planning theater parties.

Senior Citizens clubs are always eager to add interesting and stimulating sections to their clubs. The formation of theater groups has been received enthusiastically. The members attend in a body the productions planned by civic theater groups. The majority of these are most professional.

If you'd like to organize a group, you might take the following steps:

1. Send out a questionnaire to find out how many members are interested. Send details of your theater group activities to your bulletin chairman well ahead of the deadline. Another idea is to telephone all members when you are in the process of starting an activity. Lots of people will respond to a person-to-person appeal, especially when it is presented in an enthusiastic manner.

Don't be disappointed if you don't get a great number interested at first. Even five or six members can have a lot of fun, and the number will grow as word gets around.

2. Make an appointment with the manager of the civic theater group to tell him of your organization's plans to support the productions of the coming season. (Don't be shy! He'll welcome you with open arms.) He'll help you make arrangements with the ticket office to reserve a block of seats. (Have checks in hand.) You can help tremendously by accepting dates which are *not* the most popular. You'll get more preferential treatment by accepting Thursday evenings or matinee performances.

3. Plan some kind of party to precede or follow the performance. The social get-together means almost as much to the average person as the performance itself.

Here is an informal supper at the home of a member, with the schedule something like this:

6:00 P.M.:	Happy hour
7:00 P.M.:	Buffet supper
7:45 P.M.:	Quick kitchen clean-up
8:00 P.M.:	Leave for theater
8:30 P.M.:	Curtain

Make it a potluck party to avoid extra work or expense for any one person.

You might ask three persons to bring casseroles, three to bring salads, one to bring dessert, and one to bring rolls and butter.

There is bound to be food left over, and I strongly advise you to save the large bags in which food is brought and have members take home whatever is left in their casseroles or salad bowls. (This minimizes confusion and work for the hostess.) It's easy enough to tuck them away in the trunk of the car during the performance.

Here is a sample menu.

MENU

*Speedy Shrimp Supreme
Cheese Casserole
Escalloped Ham and Potato Casserole
*Party Salad
Grapefruit Aspic
Cabbage-Cucumber Salad
Hot Buttered Rolls
*Sweetie Pie Dessert
Coffee Sanka

RECIPES

SPEEDY SHRIMP SUPREME

2 ingredients

SERVES: 8

3 packages frozen rice with vegetables (I use Birdseye Rice and Peas with Mushrooms.)
1 pound shrimp, cleaned and cooked

Method:
1. Cook rice mixture according to directions on package.
2. Stir in cooked shrimp.
3. Pour into greased casserole for reheating.
4. Serve piping hot.

PARTY SALAD

4 ingredients

SERVES: 8

    1 pound lean bacon
    2 heads romaine
½–1 cup Caesar salad dressing (I use Kraft Golden Caesar
      dressing.)
    1 cup very crisp croutons (I use Kellogg's Croutettes
      Stuffing.)
    Optional: 2 hard-boiled eggs

Method:
1. Remove bacon from package without separating slices.
2. With sharp kitchen shears, cut bacon into 1-inch slices.
3. Fry all the bacon at one time in large skillet over medium heat. Stir with slotted spoon so that all pieces will be evenly brown and crisp.
4. Remove from grease with slotted spoon. Drain on paper towels. Cool.
5. Wash romaine carefully, a leaf at a time. Dry thoroughly in paper towels. Store in refrigerator.
6. Toss together lightly the romaine, bacon, and hard-boiled eggs, if desired.
7. Toss salad lightly with dressing until leaves are coated.
8. Sprinkle croutons on salad and serve at once.

SWEETIE PIE DESSERT

4 ingredients

SERVES: 8

1 8- x 9-inch prepared graham cracker crust (I use Johnson
   Fill 'n Eat Ready-Crust.)
1 7½-oz. package semisweet chocolate chips and chopped
   walnuts (I use Baker's Chips 'n Nuts.)
1 cup shredded coconut
1 cup condensed milk, not evaporated (I use Borden Eagle
   Brand Sweetened Condensed Milk.)

Method:
1. Sprinkle chocolate bits and nuts evenly on crust.
2. Pour very slowly ½ cup condensed milk over chocolate in zigzag motion.
3. Sprinkle coconut evenly over milk.
4. Pour remaining milk very slowly over coconut, using the same
   zigzag motion. The milk needn't cover the other ingredients,
   just be distributed evenly.
5. Bake in 325° oven for approximately 40 minutes, until pie is
   slightly brown around edges.
6. Cool thoroughly. Cut in 8 wedges. A small portion is sufficient
   as it is very rich.

TIPS FOR PREPARING AND SERVING   So that casserole
dishes will remain hot, cover and place in a 175° oven until serving time.

Salads should be refrigerated or covered and set in larger bowls
of crushed ice.

Rolls can be buttered and heated in an electric bun warmer or
in the oven, well wrapped in foil.

Dessert can either be in place on the table or cut into individual
servings and passed on a tray.

SETTING THE SCENE

The size of the home or apartment should determine whether to have a seated supper or a buffet. It is more comfortable and more enjoyable to sit at a dining table or at two card tables, if space is sufficient.

Attractive, colorful paper goods are available now, many with plastic coating. Because of the early curtain, we suggest that this is the way to keep KP duty to a minimum.

Winter
Parties

* ✳ *DECEMBER*
* ✿ *JANUARY*
* ❀ *FEBRUARY*

****

Bridge Luncheon

FOR 12

12:00 NOON

Most bridge players really love to play bridge, so a hostess needn't give a moment's thought to entertaining her guests.

There are many types of parties from which to choose:

A 10 o'clock breakfast with bridge following.

An 11:30 brunch with bridge before or after, or both, if they're avid players.

A 12 o'clock luncheon with bridge afterward (described here).

A 1:30 dessert and coffee with bridge following.

A 3:30 afternoon tea following bridge.

A 7:30 P.M. after-dinner coffee and dessert with bridge following.

MENU

*Cranberry Sparkle Cocktails
Salad Plate (3 small salads: *Fruit–Cream
Cheese Salad, *Stuffed Cucumber Boats,
Chicken Salad)
*Tuna Bridge Sandwiches
*Chocolate Crisps (Chocolate Covered Pretzels)
Tea

RECIPES

CRANBERRY SPARKLE COCKTAIL

4 ingredients

SERVES: 12

2 16-ounce bottles cranberry juice
2 12-ounce cans pineapple juice
1 46-ounce can grapefruit juice
1 28-ounce bottle Lemon-Lime or 7-Up
   Optional: 1 lemon, sliced thin

Method:
1. Combine drinks in punch bowl. Add ice ring or large pieces of ice.
2. Serve in cocktail glasses or punch cups. If desired, float half of a thin slice of lemon in each.

Note: To avoid diluting drinks, make rosy ice cubes of cranberry juice.

FRUIT–CREAM CHEESE SALAD

4 ingredients

YIELD: 12 pear halves

Equipment: large glass pie plate

1 15-ounce can fruit cocktail
2 1-pound cans pear halves (6 halves to a can)
1 6-ounce package cream cheese (I use Philadelphia.)
12 walnut or pecan halves

Method:
1. Drain fruit cocktail and pears, *reserving juice.*
2. Arrange fruits on several thicknesses of paper towels so that they will dry thoroughly.
3. Allow cream cheese to come to room temperature. Mash with fork. Add 1 to 2 tablespoons fruit juice, or until the cream cheese is of spreading consistency.
4. Fill the cavity of pear halves with cream cheese and spread cheese out to edges of pears. Arrange in pie plate, small ends toward the center. Press a walnut or pecan half in center of each. Place in refrigerator for 5 minutes to set slightly.
5. Remove from refrigerator and press small fruit pieces all over the cream cheese. For color, place a piece of cherry near center of each. Store, covered, in refrigerator until serving time.

STUFFED CUCUMBER BOATS

4 ingredients

SERVES : 12

    6 cucumbers
    2 10-ounce packages frozen mixed vegetables
 1½ cups mayonnaise
    1 head lettuce or romaine

Method:
1. Wash and peel cucumbers. Cut lengthwise into halves. Scoop out seeds with a spoon. Turn cucumber boats upside down to drain on paper towels.
2. Cook vegetables according to directions on package. Chill.
3. Drain vegetables. Mix with mayonnaise.
4. Fill cucumber boats and serve on greens.

TUNA BRIDGE SANDWICHES

4 ingredients

SERVES: 12

Equipment: one set card-suit cookie cutters (club, diamond, heart, and spade)

3 9¼-ounce cans white-meat tuna
1½ cups cole slaw or Thousand Island dressing
1 cup celery, diced (2 or 3 stalks)
2 loaves sandwich bread, one white, one whole wheat

Method:
Make one sandwich at a time to ensure maximum freshness.
1. Combine tuna, dressing, and celery. Mix well. Add salt and pepper if necessary.
2. Remove crusts from 1 slice white bread, and spread with tuna mixture.
3. Cut crusts from piece of dark bread and cut out center with the club cookie cutter. Set center aside for a moment. Place brown slice on top of white slice.
4. Repeat this procedure, spreading tuna on dark bread this time, and cutting club out of white bread.
5. Place white club in center of dark slice and place dark club in center of white slice.
6. Slip each into a sandwich Baggie.
7. Repeat this procedure, using the diamond, heart, and spade cutters. Allow 1 sandwich per person.

Note: These will be equally attractive and delicious with alternate fillings such as chicken salad, egg salad, ham salad, etc.

CHOCOLATE CRISPS

2 ingredients

YIELD: approximately 100

Equipment: double boiler

2 6-ounce packages chocolate bits (I use Nestle's Toll House Morsels.)

1 11-ounce package ring pretzels (I use Granny Goose. You may use bow-shaped pretzelettes if you prefer.)

Method:

1. Pour water into lower section of double boiler. Turn heat to simmer or low.
2. Pour chocolate bits into top section to melt.
3. Dip 6–8 pretzel rings at a time into chocolate sauce. Stir until well covered. Keep water in lower pan simmering all the while.
4. Lift each out with tongs or long-handled fork, allowing excess chocolate to drip back into pan.
5. Place on waxed paper to harden.

Note: These are unbelievably delicious and crisp.

TIPS FOR PREPARING AND SERVING As guests arrive, ladle cocktails into punch cups or cocktail glasses. Have cocktail napkins ready nearby.

My suggestion is to serve the lunch on metal trays which have disposable, compartmented inserts. (The ones I use are Contempo, which are attractive, inexpensive, and have available refills.)

Arrange the three salads in the large compartment, the sandwich in one of the medium compartments, two or three Chocolate Crisps in the other medium compartment, and the cup in the small one.

Arrange the trays in the kitchen and have a helper set one in front of each guest at the card tables.

After lunch the trays and cloths can be whisked away, bridge equipment substituted, and you're ready for play to begin.

SETTING THE SCENE

Be sure to limit your guest list so that the room will not be overcrowded. You should provide sturdy card tables and comfortable chairs.

If necessary to cover card tables, do so with plastic bridge covers or something which permits cards to slide easily. Provide good light, ideally a standing lamp at each table. Supply the necessary equipment for each table—two packs of fresh cards; two sharpened pencils with erasers; two score pads; individual tallies, ash trays, and matches.

ENTERTAINMENT

There is more to giving a bridge party than simply supplying guests with cards and a score pad. Here are suggestions for the thoughtful hostess. These all will add to the comfort and convenience of guests.

When extending the invitation, specify that bridge will be played. If at all possible, invite players who are fairly well matched in playing ability. Before the game starts, announce the manner of play—whether or not it's to be progressive bridge, and, if so, whether the change will come after four hands, after each rubber, or whatever.

Give at least two prizes. It could be a first and second prize, or a first and booby prize, or in the event that it is a mixed party, one prize for the high-scoring man, the other for the high-scoring woman. These should be attractively wrapped and placed in a convenient spot.

Note: The party will go smoother if the hostess doesn't play. This leaves her free to refill glasses, empty ash trays, and keep guests supplied with one thing or another. It also gives her the secure feeling of being able to fill in if necessary.

The Business Woman
Entertains at Dinner

FOR 8

7:30 to 10:30 P.M.

At one time it was unusual to find an unmarried woman much interested in her apartment. It was simply a place to hang her hat, sleep, and eat an occasional meal.

Now, however, with so much emphasis placed on decorating—color, wild prints, unusual and amusing accessories—almost every career girl is fascinated with the idea of fixing up her apartment to look just as attractive as possible. And what's the use of going to all that trouble if you can't show it off to your friends?

In addition, business women are becoming more and more interested in nutrition and the proper preparation of food. Many are considered gourmet cooks and find creative meal planning a pleasant contrast to business responsibilities.

There are any number of reasons for giving a party, such as honoring a birthday, welcoming an out-of-town guest, or introducing a new neighbor. Or you may all be attending a concert, a play, or a movie together after supper. Best of all, it may be a reunion of old friends.

Any woman can learn to be a good hostess. It's truly one of the most rewarding of all household arts. There's nothing more gay and heart-warming than a roomful of laughing, happy people.

MENU

Chilled Sherry
*Mediterranean Salad
*"Gone for the Day" Lamb Shanks in Wine
*"Gone for the Day" Lentil or Split Pea Casserole
Cornbread Muffins
*Near East "No Bake" Date Roll
Coffee

The Business Woman Entertains at Dinner   🦊   175

RECIPES

MEDITERRANEAN SALAD

4 ingredients

SERVES: 8

    1 medium Bermuda onion
    ½ cup Greek olives or pitted ripe olives
    1 8-ounce bottle Italian dressing (I use Kraft.)
    1 head lettuce
      Optional: 2 cucumbers

Method:
1. Peel and thinly slice onion into medium-sized bowl.
2. Add olives and peeled, sliced cucumbers, if desired. Pour dressing over vegetables and marinate in refrigerator for several hours or all day.
3. Break lettuce into small pieces and stir with other vegetables until well coated with dressing. This should be done just before serving.
4. Remove salad from marinade, using a large slotted spoon. Serve in bowls.

"GONE FOR THE DAY" LAMB SHANKS IN WINE

4 ingredients

SERVES: 8

Equipment: Dutch oven or large baking dish with cover

    8 pounds lamb shanks*
    2 tablespoons browning sauce (I use Kitchen Bouquet.)
    1 ⅘-ounce package garlic–French dressing mix (I use Schilling.)
    1 cup dry wine, such as Chablis, Sauterne, or other white wine

      * Choose meaty shanks with little or no fat on them.

Method:
1. Rub or brush browning sauce on lamb shanks.
2. Stir dry salad dressing mix into wine and pour over meat in Dutch oven.
3. Bake shanks covered for 30 minutes at 300°, then turn oven down to 200° and bake covered 8–10 hours (all day or all night, if preferred). You'll marvel at the tenderness and rich flavor.

Note: Casseroles of this type improve with standing, and are even more delicious made ahead and reheated an hour before serving.

"GONE FOR THE DAY" LENTIL OR SPLIT PEA CASSEROLE

4 ingredients

SERVES: 8

Equipment: large bean pot or casserole with cover

1 pound lentils, or dried split peas
2 pounds lean bulk sausage
1 package Italian dressing mix
2 10¼-ounce cans tomato soup

Method:
1. Soak lentils or split peas several hours or overnight.
2. Pour into greased bean pot or casserole.
3. Combine sausage with dressing mix, and spread on top of lentils.
4. Pour undiluted tomato soup over all. Cover.
5. Bake 8–10 hours at 200°, (all day or all night, if preferred).
6. One hour before serving, remove from oven, stir ingredients together, return to oven, and increase temperature to 225°.

Note: If you are at home while preparing this dish, stir gently every 2 or 3 hours.

NEAR EAST "NO BAKE" DATE ROLL

4 ingredients

SERVES : 8 to 10

1 8-ounce package chopped dates (I use Dromedary.)
2 cups soft miniature marshmallows
3 cups graham cracker crumbs
½ pint heavy cream for whipping

Method:
1. Mix together the dates and marshmallows.
2. Set aside 2 tablespoons graham cracker crumbs.
3. Add remaining crumbs to date mixture.
4. Mix thoroughly with hands as if you were making bread, until the mixture forms a ball. If mixture tends to be crumbly, add a little water, 1 tablespoon at a time, until it sticks together. The outside of the ball should feel tacky.
5. Sprinkle the reserved 2 tablespoons of cracker crumbs on a bread board and roll back and forth until you have a roll approximately 3 inches in diameter and 6 inches long.
6. Wrap in Saran Wrap and chill in refrigerator for 12 or more hours.
7. Whip the cream shortly before serving. Cut the roll in ¾-inch slices and serve with unsweetened whipped cream.

TIPS FOR PREPARING AND SERVING   The menu for 8 is a perfect one for the girl who works all day. Everything is prepared the night before. On the day of the party, both the Lamb Shanks in Wine and the Lentil Casserole cook all day in a very slow oven. You just can't imagine how tender and flavorful these long-cooking dishes are as opposed to food which cooks at a high temperature.

The Mediterranean Salad marinates in the refrigerator all day.

The Date Roll is so easy, you won't believe it—no baking involved, just combining four ingredients and rolling the dough back and forth a few times between your hands.

Have wine glasses ready on a tray in the kitchen with cocktail napkins. When guests arrive, pour chilled sherry into wine glasses. Carry tray to living room and invite each guest to take a glass and napkin.

Place casseroles on top shelf of a rolling cart and serve at table.

Spoon salad into bowls, and place before each guest.

Reheat cornbread muffins in oven.

Slice Date Roll Dessert an hour or two in advance, arrange on serving plate and enclose all in a Baggie, foil, or Saran Wrap to keep fresh. Place on second shelf of cart along with dessert plates, forks, and a bowl of whipped cream to pass.

Used plates can be placed on bottom shelf of cart, and dessert served without leaving the table.

SETTING THE SCENE

Even in a small apartment there is room for two card tables and for folding chairs. Keep these in a convenient place where they can be whisked out and set up at the last moment.

The night before, place on a tray the necessary table-setting equipment: tablecloth and napkins, silverware, china, glasses, salts and peppers, cream pitchers and sugar bowls, cups and saucers.

Just before serving, open the folding tables, place cloths on them, bring in the tray and say, "Who wants the honor of setting the tables?" Don't be surprised if all say, "I do!" My guess is that they'll set it together in a matter of moments. If you want the occasion to be especially festive, have bouquets and candles nearby to be set in centers of tables.

Christmas Eve Dinner

FOR 12

6 :30 to 9 :00 P.M.

Although many family traditions are not held in the same reverence they once were, there is an exception : Christmas. Most of us enjoy preparing for it in the same way, year after year—the Christmas tree in the same place ; the same carefully packed ornaments and strings of lights ; the same way of decorating the house ; the same menu ; the same after-dinner games ; and the same dear familiar carols.

By repeating these nostalgic customs, we seem to recapture that glow, excitement, and good will that is mysteriously reborn each Christmas Eve.

Sharing Christmas with everyone in your family, from six-week-old Johnny to 95-year-old Great-Grandmother, can be one of the most rewarding privileges in life.

Christmas Eve is surely the most magical night of the year, with young ones home from school, house guests arriving for the holidays, the sight of Christmas lights blinking on the tree, the sound of well-beloved carols, the smell of pine on the mantel, and the squealing joy of excited tots gazing at the mysterious pile of colorfully wrapped presents around the tree.

Many families prefer having their big holiday dinner and gift opening on Christmas Eve, leaving Christmas Day free for callers and church services.

Following is a very nice menu, with few last-minute preparations.

MENU

*Chicken Egg Drop Soup
*Standing Rib Roast of Beef *Creamy Horseradish Sauce
*Speedy Blender Yorkshire Puddings
*Scalloped Corn en Casserole
*Yule Logs
Coffee   Milk

RECIPES

CHICKEN EGG DROP SOUP

2 ingredients

SERVES: 12

4 eggs
6 10½-ounce cans chicken broth (I use Campbell's.)

Method:
1. Beat eggs until light.
2. Heat chicken broth, with 6 cans water, to a slow boil.
3. Pour beaten eggs into broth in a steady, slow stream. It will immediately form fine threads.
4. Serve at once.

STANDING RIB ROAST OF BEEF

2 ingredients

SERVES: 12

Equipment: shallow roasting pan; meat thermometer

6–8 pound standing rib roast (choice grade)
2 teaspoons herb-seasoned salt (I use Lawry's Pinch of Herbs.)

Method:
The following method of cooking this roast should be called Business Woman's Delight! It is *that* easy and the meat is oh, so tender.
In the morning:
1. Preheat oven to 375°.

2. Place roast, fat side up, in shallow roasting pan. Sprinkle herb-seasoned salt over meat. Insert meat thermometer in center of fleshy section of roast.
3. Roast the beef for 1 hour. Turn off heat. Do *not* open oven door.
4. One hour before serving time in evening, turn oven once again to 375°. Roast 45 minutes. Remove from oven and let rest 15 minutes. The meat thermometer should register 150°. This is for medium rare, which the majority of people favor. Allow to roast slightly longer for medium, but do not overcook. This robs the roast of tenderness and flavor. Serve with Creamy Horseradish Sauce.

CREAMY HORSERADISH SAUCE

3 ingredients

SERVES : 6

    1 pint dairy sour cream
½–1 cup prepared horseradish (according to taste)
    2 tablespoons chopped onion

Method:
1. Combine ingredients.
2. Store in refrigerator.

Note: There's a delicious prepared product now on the market, simply called "Horseradish Sauce" by Kraft.

SPEEDY BLENDER YORKSHIRE PUDDINGS

4 ingredients

YIELD : 12 popovers

Equipment: custard cups or heavy popover pans similar to muffin tins; electric blender

4 tablespoons butter (½ stick)
3–5 eggs (¾ cup)
1½ cups milk
1½ cups flour (I use Gold Medal Wondra Quick Mixing All-Purpose Flour.)

Method:
1. Place 1 teaspoon butter in each custard cup.
2. Set cups on cookie sheet and heat in 375° oven for about 10 minutes.
3. Break eggs into blender. Add milk and flour. Run blender 2 or 3 seconds. Turn off. Turn on again for 2 or 3 seconds.
4. Remove hot custard cups from oven and fill them halfway.
5. Bake at 375° about 40 minutes. They should be puffed up and golden. Remove from oven and, with sharp knife, cut slit in side of each to let steam escape.
6. Return to oven and bake an additional 10 minutes.

Note: The recipe for popovers and Yorkshire pudding is basically the same, except that Yorkshire pudding is usually baked in a pan about 8 inches square. I personally prefer the individual ones because there is an abundance of nice crisp crust and less chance of a doughy middle. They are delicious either with gravy or eaten out of hand with lots of butter.

   If perchance they have to wait dinner, don't worry. Turn them upside down so that the bottoms won't steam and leave them in oven with the oven door open.

SCALLOPED CORN *en* CASSEROLE

4 ingredients

SERVES : 12

Equipment: 3-quart casserole

3 cups stuffing mix (I use Kellogg's Croutettes Stuffing.)
3 eggs
3 12-ounce cans Mexicorn
3 10½-ounce cans white sauce (approximately 1 quart)

Method:
1. Set aside 1 cup of stuffing mix.
2. Beat eggs. Add drained corn and white sauce to 2 cups stuffing mix.
3. Pour into greased casserole.
4. Chop the remaining 1 cup of stuffing mix into crumbs. Sprinkle on top of corn mixture.
5. Bake 20 minutes at 375°, until bubbling hot.

YULE LOGS

4 ingredients

YIELD : 3 dozen

Equipment: cookie sheet

1 cup confectioner's sugar (½ cup is reserved for coating the cookies)
1 cup margarine (2 sticks)
2½ cups all-purpse flour (I use Gold Medal Wondra Quick Mixing Flour.)
1½ cups walnuts, finely chopped

Method:

1. Set aside ½ cup confectioner's sugar. This will be used later.
2. Allow margarine to come to room temperature.
3. Combine margarine, ½ cup confectioner's sugar, flour, nuts, and 2 teaspoons water. Knead with hands as if you were making bread. The warmth of your hands helps in attaining the right consistency. The dough should be soft enough to form a ball. If it is too crumbly add another teaspoon of water.
4. Roll a small amount of dough, about the size of a walnut, into a ball between palms of hands, then back and forth between your fingers, so that it resembles a small log about 3 inches long (¼ cup of dough makes 4 logs). Continue until all dough is used.
5. Place on ungreased cookie sheet, about ½ inch apart. Set them in refrigerator until chilled.
6. Bake in 350° oven 15–18 minutes, until crisp and slightly browned.
7. Cool thoroughly, then roll in remaining ½ cup confectioner's sugar.

TIPS FOR PREPARING AND SERVING   Egg Drop Soup is in place when family and guests are called to dinner.

Father carves Roast Beef and serves a portion, then passes, family style, to Mother.

Mother serves Yorkshire Puddings and Scalloped Corn, then passes to guest of honor, at Father's right. Continue around table.

Hoseradish Sauce is spooned into medium-sized bowl ahead of time and passed at table.

Yule Logs can be passed at table after main course plates are removed.

Coffee can be served throughout meal, or later with the Yule Log cookies.

SETTING THE SCENE

There is an almost endless selection of shapes, colors, and prices of Christmas decorations. Most appealing, however, is the simple homemade variety which every member of the family helps to fashion.

Such a project is this spectacular 6-foot wreath for your picture window, which will send out warm greetings throughout the Christmas season. You'll need:

> A 15-foot length of chicken wire
> Strings of Christmas lights—all one color, or in two colors (my favorites are blue and green lights); or you may use all the colors in the rainbow
> Short, fresh evergreen twigs or holly, or a combination of both
> A heavy-duty, outdoor extension cord

Roll chicken wire into a tubelike form, then secure ends with wire so that it resembles a wreath. This operation works best flat on the floor or on the lawn. Attach a heavy wire loop so that it can be suspended from a strong hook above the window. Some people find it easier to hang the wreath and then stuff in the greens. If you prefer doing it flat, don't forget that it will be very heavy when finished and will probably take two men to lift it and attach it to the hook.

Wire Christmas lights to the wreath. Place them as close to each other as you wish. The more lights, the more dramatic it will be. Plan so that the terminal plug will be as close as possible to the source of electrical supply. Usually you'll need an extension cord.

Have ready a large number of evergreen sprigs, or in tropical areas any greenery which lasts well out of water. Insert greenery into the chicken wire at all angles until you have a solid green wreath. (Often you can buy separate boughs, or even an extra Christmas tree that may be selling cheap because of being lopsided or otherwise undesirable—just so long as it is good and fresh.)

Centerpieces are seldom meant to be eaten, but here's an exception. It's meant to be enjoyed with before-dinner drinks.

At the ten-cent store buy a styrofoam tree (cone shape) about 15 inches tall and 6 inches in diameter at the base. Glue it to a heavy wooden base so that when it is loaded, it won't topple over. Then cover the whole thing with tinfoil. Decorate it with olives, cheese cubes, radishes, inch lengths of franks, pickles, and cherry tomatoes, using toothpicks. Then fill in with parsley, which also fastens on very simply with toothpicks.

A food tree is a gay thing to put on the coffee table at Christmas time.

ENTERTAINMENT

Watching the children opening their presents, and unwrapping your own, must surely be the best entertainment there is.

Gathering around the piano to sing the old familiar carols and other Christmas songs runs a close second. Here are 12 favorites:

"Silent Night"
"Joy to the World"
"Adeste, Fideles"
"Good King Wenceslas"
"O Little Town of Bethlehem"
"It Came Upon the Midnight Clear"
"White Christmas"
"Frosty, the Snowman"
"Rudolph, the Red-Nosed Reindeer"
"Winter Wonderland"
"Jingle Bells"
"Santa Claus Is Coming to Town"

Annual New Year's Eve Eggnog Party

FOR 48

8:00 P.M. TO 12:00 MIDNIGHT

A friend of ours holds open house each New Year's Eve from 8 o'clock until midnight, and it is one of the highlights of the holiday season in our city.

Her home is one of the few authentic Spanish haciendas remaining in this area. As you enter through the 8-foot, heavily carved doors, it seems as if you've turned the clock back a hundred years.

It is a very special party to all of her friends, and most of us take special pains to dress for the occasion.

Invitations are extended in an informal, casual manner. On her Christmas card, underneath her signature, she writes simply, "Eggnog, Dec. 31, 8–12 o'clock. Regrets only."

One of the appealing features is that you may stay for as long or as short a time as you wish. Many friends drop in for half an hour on their way to a club dance. Others stop by on their way home from a dinner party. If guests have no other plans for the evening, they are welcome to stay for 2 or 3 hours. There is no pressure one way or the other.

Most of us are not equipped to give a party such as this, but the idea is an excellent one and it can be copied on a smaller scale. An advantage of this type of party is that it can be given on the spur of the moment, particularly if you still have some of your holiday baking left.

It really is a very pleasant way to see a number of your friends and to give them an hour or two of pleasure on this very exciting night.

MENU

*Holiday Eggnog
Small, Open-Faced Sandwiches
Tiny Biscuits with Thin Slices of Ham and Mustard Sauce
*Hot Crab Nippies
*Filled Swedish Cookies
*Orange-Glazed Walnuts
Fruitcake
Coffee

RECIPES

HOLIDAY EGGNOG

4 ingredients

YIELD : 24 punch cups*

6 eggs
1 cup sugar
1 quart Half-and-Half
1 quart bourbon (Some prefer brandy, some rum.)
Optional: grated nutmeg

> *Estimate about 3 punch cups per guest. Make eggnog ahead and store in large containers in the refrigerator.

Method:

1. Separate the eggs.
2. Beat eggs together with ½ cup sugar for about 30 seconds, preferably with an electric beater. Rinse and dry beater.
3. Beat whites with the remaining ½ cup sugar in another large bowl until very stiff. Fold thoroughly into yolks.
4. Stir in Half-and-Half.
5. Add bourbon and stir.
6. Chill thoroughly.
7. At serving time, pour into large punch bowl. Serve in punch cups, preferably glass, with a sprinkle of nutmeg, if desired.

HOT CRAB NIPPIES

4 ingredients

YIELD: approximately 8 dozen canapés

Equipment: cookie sheet

- 2 loaves white sandwich bread
- 2 7½-ounce cans white crabmeat*
- ½ cup mayonnaise (I use Best Foods.)
- ¼ pound sharp cheddar cheese (about 2 cups when grated)

  * Buy best quality available.

Method:
1. Cut crusts from bread. Place under broiler to toast one side.
2. Pick over crabmeat, removing bony tissues, if any.
3. Combine crabmeat and mayonnaise. Spread on untoasted side of bread.
4. Grate cheese. Sprinkle generously on crab mixture.
5. Place on cookie sheet. Broil 3 inches from heat until cheese is melted and edges of bread are slightly toasted.
6. Cut each slice from corner to corner, and then cut again to make 4 triangular canapés. Serve at once.

FILLED SWEDISH COOKIES

4 ingredients

YIELD: 3 dozen

Equipment: cookie sheet

- 1 cup butter
- ½ cup confectioner's sugar
- 2 cups all-purpose flour
- ¼ cup raspberry jelly (or any jam or marmalade of your choice)

  Optional: nuts, finely chopped

Method:
1. Preheat oven to 350°.
2. Let butter come to room temperature.
3. Mix together butter, sugar, and flour. Knead, and work together with hands until it forms a ball. If crumbly, add 1 tablespoon water.*
4. Pinch off small pieces of dough and roll into balls about 1 inch in diameter. Arrange on cookie sheet.
5. Bake for 5 minutes. Remove from oven. With a thimble, make a small depression in top of each cookie.
6. Return to oven and bake an additional 15–20 minutes or until light brown around edges. Cool.
7. Fill depressions with jelly or jam. If you wish, fill half of the cookies with jelly, half with marmalade. (You'll need only a small amount in each, approximately ¼ teaspoon.)
If you wish, sprinkle finely chopped nuts on top of jelly.

* Room temperature has an effect on the consistency of baked goods. In cold weather, it may be necessary to add water; in warm weather, the consistency may be just right.

ORANGE-GLAZED WALNUTS

4 ingredients

YIELD : 100 walnut halves, approximately

¾ cup sugar
 4 tablespoons orange juice
 1 teaspoon grated orange rind
2½ cups walnut halves, shelled

Method:
1. Combine sugar, orange juice, and orange rind in saucepan. Blend thoroughly.
2. Cook over low heat, stirring occasionally, until the syrup registers 238° on a candy thermometer. (Another test is to drop a teaspoonful of syrup in cold water. When it forms a ball, it is ready.)
3. Remove from heat and add walnuts. Stir lightly to coat the nuts with glaze.
4. Turn out at once on waxed paper and separate with forks. Cool completely.
5. Store in covered container in cool place.

TIPS FOR PREPARING AND SERVING   The various goodies are arranged tastefully on silver platters and footed cake stands. Paper doilies are used under the various food items. A stack of salad plates, each with a small doily to set the cup on, is placed near the punch bowl. The server sets the punch cup on the doily and asks each guest if he wishes a sprinkle of nutmeg. Guests choose what they want in the way of food and place it on the other side of plate.

SETTING THE SCENE

Probably one of the reasons that people enjoy this party so much is that it is done in the "grand manner," a feature seldom encountered these days. With little household help available, we appreciate all the more those little gracious touches that are so rare. We all enjoy a little pampering occasionally.

When guests pull up into the courtyard of this lovely home, they are met by an attendant who opens the car doors, then parks the car. A jovial butler throws open the door, bids them a good evening, then directs guests to rooms set aside for wraps.

To the right of the entrance hall is a large living room with a handsome fireplace along one wall. Here our hostess, in a floor-length hostess gown, receives her guests. After chatting for a few moments with each one, she directs guests to the dining room where her table is extended to its full length to make room for all the goodies offered. The table is covered with a magnificent linen and lace banquet cloth.

At one end of the table is a very large silver punch bowl for the eggnog. (This is the most delicious eggnog I've ever tasted. I'm very grateful to her that she kindly shared her recipe with me.)

At the opposite end of the table is a large silver coffee and tea service. The buffet table is truly a "groaning board."

ENTERTAINMENT

For this party, the hostess engages a small group of musicians, in Spanish and Mexican costumes, who provide background music during the evening.

All the well-loved Spanish and Mexican melodies are featured, in addition to American-Mexican songs such as "In Old Monterey," "In a Little Spanish Town," "Ramona," "Marcheta," "Vaya con Dios," "Blue Spanish Eyes," etc.

The dining room is lighted almost entirely by candles, which gives such a glamorous atmosphere to holiday parties.

"My Funny Valentine" Supper

FOR 16

7:00 to 11:00 P.M.

When I was one-and-twenty,
I heard a wise man say,
"Give crowns and pounds and guineas
But not your heart away;
Give pearls away and rubies
But keep your fancy free."
But I was one-and-twenty,
No use to talk to me.

The above saying may be a wise one, but oh, what a dull world this would be if we all followed this advice.

The young in heart from sixteen to sixty will adore getting an invitation to a Valentine Party. Hearts and flowers and Cupids and darts are as much in vogue today as at the turn of the century.

However, for a change of pace, we decided to use the comic Valentine theme instead of the usual sentimental type. Richard Rodgers' "My Funny Valentine" provided the inspiration for this fun party. It turned out to be a hilarious affair, and may suggest ideas for your own Valentine Party.

Here is the invitation:

Most valentine parties are sugar and spice,
Hearts and flowers and everything nice.
Our valentine party is strictly for fun—
You can act the clown or simpleton.
Though your face and figure are really divine,
Please come as a funny valentine.

This proved to be one of the easiest of all themes to work with, from point of view of both hostess and guest. Several couples came as well-known comic strip characters. There were Charlie Brown and Lucy; Li'l Abner and Daisy Mae Yokum; the Flintstones; Dick Tracy and Liz. Several arrived in clown costume. Others were comical in mismatched clothing. Several came in hobo costumes; others featured shipwreck attire.

MENU

*Margaritas   Guacamole Dip   Frito Chips
*South-of-the-Border Stuffed Tomatoes
*Viva Chicken Tortillas
Rice with Mushrooms and Peas
Beer
Mexican Wedding Cakes
Coffee

RECIPES

MARGARITAS

3 ingredients

YIELD: 24 cocktails (approximately)

1 fifth tequila
2 fifths Margarita mix (I use Trader Vic.)
½ cup salt (The cocktail glass rim is dampened slightly and
  dipped lightly into the salt.)

Method:

To make in a blender:

1. Pour in ½ cup tequila.
2. Add 1 cup Margarita mix.
3. Add 2 cups chipped ice and blend.
4. The ideal method is to chill the cocktail glasses in the freezer compartment, so that they have a lovely frost on them. Then dip the rim in salt, then return to freezer. In this way you have a thin crust of salt. Remove each glass just before serving and pour the liquid almost to the top.

Note: These are about as strong as Martinis, but *taste* mild. Beware!

SOUTH-OF-THE-BORDER STUFFED TOMATOES

4 ingredients

SERVES: 8*

    4 large, ripe tomatoes (½ tomato per person)
    2 packages frozen peas
   12 stuffed green olives
    1 cup mayonnaise
      Optional: 4 tablespoons chopped sweet pickle

*For 16, the recipe will have to be made up twice. The recipe for 8 is easier to handle.

Method:

1. Wash tomatoes and cut in half horizontally. Remove pulp and discard. Refrigerate tomatoes.
2. Cook peas according to directions on package. Do not overcook!
3. Gently toss together chopped green olives, peas, mayonnaise, and chopped pickle if you wish. Refrigerate.
4. Just before serving, spoon the mixture into the tomato shells.

VIVA CHICKEN TORTILLAS

4 ingredients

SERVES : 8*

Equipment: 9- x 13-inch baking dish

4 whole chicken breasts†
8 corn tortillas
1 7-ounce can chili salsa sauce (I use Ortega Green Chili
   Salsa.)
2 cans undiluted cheddar cheese soup (I use Campbell's.)

*For 16, the recipe will have to be made up twice, using two
9- x 13-inch baking dishes.
†Buy large meaty ones.

Method:
1. Simmer chicken in 2 cups water approximately 30 minutes or
   until you can easily remove bones and skin. Reserve the broth.
2. Cut each breast in half again. Make a layer of chicken in 9- x
   13-inch baking dish.
3. Lay tortillas in a stack, the way they come in the package. Cut
   them into 8 wedges as though you were cutting a pie in 8 pieces.
4. Arrange tortilla pieces on top of chicken pieces.
5. Mix chili salsa with 2 cans cheddar cheese soup and the reserved
   chicken broth. Pour over the chicken and tortillas.
6. Bake 1–1½ hours at 300°.

TIPS FOR PREPARING AND SERVING   Margaritas can be
made ahead in blender or punch bowl. Add ice later.

Pour Guacamole Dip into a bowl. Have Frito chips nearby for
dunking.

Set Stuffed Tomatoes at each place. When guests are seated,
hostess begins on salad so that others may start, then leaves to get
the main course on the table. I strongly advise asking a friend in
advance to help with this. She could also remove salad plates.

For the Chicken Tortillas and Rice with Mushrooms and Peas, let's take a hint from Mexican restaurants, who "dish up" in the kitchen on hot, hot plates and rush them right to the table.

Serve dessert after the main course plates have been removed to kitchen. Set small butter plate in front of each guest, and pass the Mexican Wedding Cakes.

Make coffee in large 30-cup coffeemaker before guests arrive. Set it on separate table and guests serve themselves when ready.

SETTING THE SCENE

Table covering can be two striped beach towels in red, white, and green, Mexico's national colors. Place the towels diagonally to resemble serapes.

China may be white pottery and glassware, dark green goblets.

For a centerpiece, use a wooden cart hitched to a ceramic donkey. The cart is overflowing with small, colorful vegetables such as radishes, string beans, shelled lima beans, tiny carrots, brussels sprouts, and tiny red chili peppers. Use any or all of these. They are striking and unusual even in a wicker basket.

Green peppers hold tall red candles. Cut a hole in the top of each with an apple corer. If pepper doesn't sit evenly, cut a small slice from bottom. Some people prefer turning the bell pepper upside down, then cutting the hole for the candle. Here, too, the underside may have to be trimmed slightly so that it will stand straight.

ENTERTAINMENT

Look for old-fashioned comic valentines in a ten-cent store. These only cost about a penny each. They are the highly insulting variety which kids at one time passed around. Put them in two paper bags, one group suitable for the women and one for the men. Pass at table and, without peeking, have each guest take one and read it aloud.

Examples:

For the women: *It's true you're wearing a pretty gown,*
                  But you'll never win a beauty crown!

For the men: *You're dark and handsome, but what a bore!*
                  You'll always remain a bachelor!

LOVE STORY   Here's a game that is fun to play and requires little advance preparation. Have on hand a piece of construction paper about 18 x 24 inches. Ask for players to call out titles of well-known songs. Write the titles down as they are called. Get at least 35 song titles. Now explain that your guests, in teams of 4 each, are to compose a love story made up of the titles they have chosen. There can be no more than 3 connecting words between titles. Each team uses the same list of songs. Your story could go something like this:

Frankie and Johnny were *Drifting and Dreaming* while *Cruising down the River on a Sunday Afternoon. "Oh Johnny, Oh Johnny, Put Your Arms Around Me, Honey* and *Gimme a Little Kiss, Will Ya Huh?* Come on, *Cuddle up a Little Closer.* I need *Someone to Watch over Me."* Replied Johnny, *"I Got Plenty of Nothin'* except *Blues in the Night. I'm Always Chasing Rainbows.* We'd be *Feudin' and Fightin' 'Til the End of Time. Don't Fence Me in."*

This will give you the idea. Don't forget—the cornier the better.

GREAT LOVERS CHARADES   Slips containing the names of famous lovers have been placed in a bowl. A table nearby is supplied with props such as false moustaches, daggers, guns, tree branches, cardboard moon, paper roses, hats, capes, fans, a hobby horse, etc. Any or all of these may be used.

Couples take turns, first one team and then the other, selecting a slip from the bowl. They get a quick look at it, select props, then immediately start acting without discussing it with one another. A limit of 2 minutes is given.

Suggestions: Adam and Eve; Anthony and Cleopatra; Punch and Judy; Romeo and Juliet; Napoleon Bonaparte and Josephine; Robert Browning and Elizabeth Barrett; Prince Albert and Queen Victoria; Casanova and Friend; Don Quixote and Dulcinea, etc.

Mardi Gras Company Dinner

7:00 to 10:00 P.M.

To be "way down yonder in New Orleans" is exciting at any time of year, but particularly so at Mardi Gras time. The contagious gaiety of the masked revelers, the unmatched pageantry and color of the costumed parades, the sightseeing around the mighty Mississippi Delta, and, possibly best of all, the places to dine, all beckon to bring one back again and again.

The Mardi Gras theme is becoming a popular one, both for club parties and home entertaining.

MENU

Ramos Gin Fizzes
*Deviled Clams
*Celery Victor Salad Plate
*Steak Diane
Duchess Potatoes
Spinach Soufflé
*Florentines
*Café Brûlot

Mardi Gras Company Dinner   201

RECIPES

DEVILED CLAMS

4 ingredients

SERVES : 6

Equipment: 6 baking shells or individual casseroles

- 2 cans chopped clams
- 1 cup creamy onion salad dressing* (I use Wishbone.)
- 10–12 crackers
- 2 tablespoons melted butter

   *Thousand Island dressing may be substituted.

Method:
1. Drain clams. Combine clams and dressing.
2. Spoon into buttered shells or six individual casseroles.
3. Chop or roll crackers fine. Combine cracker crumbs with melted butter.
4. Sprinkle buttered cracker crumbs over clam mixture.
5. Bake uncovered in hot, 400° oven for 10 minutes or until crumbs are slightly browned and mixture is bubbling hot.

CELERY VICTOR SALAD PLATE

4 ingredients

SERVES : 6

Equipment: skillet; flat baking dish

- 3 stalks of hearts of celery
- 1 8-ounce bottle French or Caesar dressing (I use Kraft Golden Caesar Dressing.)
- 1 cup black olives, pitted
- 1 2-ounce jar pimientos, sliced
  Optional: shredded lettuce

Method:
1. Cut each stalk in half lengthwise, without separating the stalks. Cut across the stalk, leaving approximately 6 inches of stem. (Save the tops for soups, stews, salads, etc.)
2. Wash celery and place in skillet or pot so that it lies flat. Pour water over it to cover, and simmer about 20 minutes, or until fork-tender. Drain.
3. Transfer carefully with broad spatula to flat container. A 9- x 13-inch baking dish is good.
4. Pour dressing on celery and allow to marinate, turning occasionally, until it is well chilled. Marinate ripe olives at same time.
5. Arrange on salad plate, over shredded lettuce if desired. Garnish with strips of pimiento and black olives.

STEAK DIANE

4 ingredients

SERVES : 6

Equipment: heavy, large skillet

2 tablespoons butter (not margarine)
6 fillets of beef tenderloin (filet mignon), cut 1 inch thick
1 teaspoon mixed herbs (I use Lawry's Pinch of Herbs.)
1 cup dairy sour cream
   Optional: 2 tablespoons mustard or A-1 Sauce

Method:
1. Melt butter in skillet over medium-high heat.
2. Sauté beef fillets in butter about 2 minutes per side. They should be nicely browned on outside and pink inside. Transfer to warm platter. Keep warm in low oven for the minute or two it takes to make sauce.
3. Stir herbs into sour cream. Add mustard sauce or A-1 Sauce if desired.
4. Mix sour cream mixture with pan drippings. Cook at low temperature for about one minute, stirring all the while.
5. Pour sauce over steaks, and serve at once piping hot.

FLORENTINES

4 ingredients

YIELD: 20 confections (half-cookie, half-candy)

Equipment: 9- x 13-inch cookie sheet; aluminum foil

20 square graham crackers
 1 6–8-ounce package sliced almonds
 1 cup dark brown sugar
 ¾ cup butter

Method:
1. Preheat oven to 400°.
2. Line cookie sheet completely with foil.
3. Place graham crackers on cookie sheet.
4. Sprinkle nuts over graham crackers.
5. Boil the brown sugar and butter together for exactly 3 minutes. Pour at once over nuts.
6. Bake in 400° oven for *exactly* 7 minutes.
7. Cut into squares while still hot. Cool.
8. Remove from foil and arrange on serving dish.

CAFÉ BRÛLOT

4 ingredients

YIELD: 6 coffee cupfuls or 12 demitasse cupfuls

Equipment: chafing dish and 6 demitasse cups and saucers

 5 cups strong coffee
12 whole cloves
 1 orange (peel only)
 1 cup coffee-flavored brandy
    Optional: 6 cinnamon sticks to use as stirrers

Method:
1. Place 8 tablespoons of coffee in percolator.
2. Add 12 whole cloves and thinly sliced orange peel. Allow to go through the regular cycle.
3. At serving time, half fill the bottom section of chafing dish with hot water. Light the Sterno or alcohol. Pour brandy into top section of chafing dish. Have in readiness the freshly made coffee.
4. Ignite the brandy when it begins to simmer. Dip a ladle into the mixture and lift a little of it high in the air. A ribbon of golden-blue flame follows the motion and is a sight to thrill even the most sophisticated. Allow to burn only a few moments.
5. Pour in the coffee slowly. The flames will flicker, then die. Serve, preferably in demitasse cups. Place a cinnamon stick in each, if desired.

TIPS ON PREPARING AND SERVING   Ramos Gin Fizzes are traditionally served in a tall thin glass. Parfait glasses are fine.

As soon as guests are seated at table, place a sizzling hot baking dish or shell of Deviled Clams in front of each.

Celery Victor can be set above each place before calling guests to dinner. Crescent-shaped salad plates are most practical when serving salad with dinner because they curve around the plate, thus taking up less room.

Steak Diane is a dish which is fun to prepare at table under the admiring eyes of your guests. Place an electric skillet on the top shelf of a serving cart with ingredients nearby.

Vegetables can be kept on an electric hot tray on second shelf of cart along with hot plates.

Place two Florentines on each dessert plate before guests arrive. Serve with coffee.

Serve Café Brûlot in small coffee cups. Place cinnamon stick in each, if desired.

SETTING THE SCENE

Because Mardi Gras is practically synonymous with carnival, you can let your imagination run riot in regard to using bright colors and flamboyant accessories.

I use a very gay tablecloth made of bright material, the type usually used for costumes. It has a white background with shiny pin stripes of vivid Mardi Gras jewel colors—emerald green, sapphire blue, amethyst, and ruby red. The napkins I use are in solid colors—one red, one blue, one green, etc.

As an underskirt, I use a fitted bottom twin sheet on a 36- x 72-inch table. Corners of sheet fit securely over corners of table.

Nine tall candles in various colors are secured in ten-cent store holders and arranged in a serpentine design at the back of the table. Bases are covered with greens and serpentine ribbon confetti. China is white with a dark blue border. Backdrop decorations pinned to the draperies are large glamour masks and butterflies made of construction paper and trimmed with sequins and glitter.

Index

Mardi Gras company dinner, 201–206

Margaritas, 195–96

Marinated fresh vegetables, 31

Meat
  barbecued cheeseburgers, 95–96
  carving, 11, 12
  chili dogs, 82–83
  lamb shanks in wine, 176–77
  miniature open-faced broiled hamburgers, 76
  roast filet of beef sandwiches, 134–35
  spaghetti and meatball casserole, 88–89
  spareribs in "open pit" barbecue sauce, 30
  standing rib roast of beef, 181–82
  steak Diane, 203
  Texas jailhouse stew, 146–47
  see also Poultry

Meatballs: spaghetti and meatball casserole, 88–89

Mediterranean salad, 176

Menus
  anniversary open house, 74
  bachelor lunch, 134
  bridge luncheon, 169
  business woman's dinner, 175
  children's midsummer African safari supper, 87
  Christmas Eve dinner, 180
  cocktails and buffet supper, 139
  Easter lunch, 50
  Father's Day picnic in the park, 95
  Fourth of July reunion supper, 102–103
  garden wedding and reception, 115
  hobo supper for Halloween, 145
  home-cooked lunch, 134
  Indian birthday supper, 82
  Mardi Gras company dinner, 201
  midsummer tropical luau, 122–23
  Mother's Day breakfast, 60
  "My Funny Valentine" supper, 195
  New Year's Eve eggnog party, 189

St. Patrick's Day supper, 30
  stork shower, 65
  Sunday brunch, 44–45
  supper shower for bride and groom, 38
  Thanksgiving dinner, 155
  theater supper for senior citizens, 163

Meringue: chocolate mint, 67

Midsummer tropical luau, 122–29

Mincemeat coffee cakes, 48

Miniature open-faced broiled hamburgers, 76

Mints, 117

Mixed fruit compote, 60–61

Morning coffee party, 64–70

Mother's Day breakfast in the garden, 60–63

Muffin tin 15-minute breakfast, 61–62

Mushroom-egg scallop, 46

Music for parties, 23–24, 80, 121, 129

"My Funny Valentine" supper, 194–200

Near East "no bake" date roll, 178

Neighborhood party, 8

Name tags for parties, 8

New Year's Eve eggnog party, 188–93

Nibblers: "Nuts and bolts," 38

"No bake" Near East date roll, 178

Nuts
  fruit-cream cheese salad, 170–71
  nut and coconut macaroons, 67–68
  nut-coated chicken breasts, 51
  nutty brown bread half moons, 76–77
  orange-glazed walnuts, 191–92

"Nuts and bolts" nibblers, 38

Oatmeal cookies, date-filled, 135–36

Obstacle course game, 91–92

Old-fashioned potato salad, 96–97

One-bite chicken rolls, 115–16

Orange-glazed walnuts, 191–92

Oriental fruit sauce, 52

Outdoor parties, 12